CAMBRIDGE BOOKS

1521–1800

A LIST OF BOOKS
PRINTED IN CAMBRIDGE
AT THE
UNIVERSITY PRESS
1521–1800

CAMBRIDGE
AT THE UNIVERSITY PRESS
1935

CAMBRIDGE UNIVERSITY PRESS
Cambridge, New York, Melbourne, Madrid, Cape Town, Singapore,
São Paulo, Delhi, Dubai, Tokyo, Mexico City

Cambridge University Press
The Edinburgh Building, Cambridge CB2 8RU, UK

Published in the United States of America by Cambridge University Press, New York

www.cambridge.org
Information on this title: www.cambridge.org/9780521155410

First published 1935
First paperback edition 2010

A catalogue record for this publication is available from the British Library

ISBN 978-0-521-04108-9 Hardback
ISBN 978-0-521-15541-0 Paperback

NOTE

THIS LIST is a composite work. The first part, 1521–1650, was compiled by the late Francis Jenkinson and was included in Robert Bowes' *Catalogue of Cambridge Books* (1894). Some additions were made and the list was continued to 1750 by Mr S. C. Roberts, who included it as an Appendix in his *History of the Cambridge University Press* (1921). Since then the *Short-Title Catalogue of English Books*, 1475–1640, has appeared, and it has been my first task to check the early entries against it. I am glad to say that this work has resulted on the one hand in some thirty additions to Jenkinson's list, and on the other in the discovery of seven new titles which Dr A. W. Pollard has accepted for the *Short-Title Catalogue*.

In the period 1641–1750 I have identified some two dozen books hitherto listed as doubtful, and have added about a dozen new titles.

My second task has been to continue the List from 1751 to 1800. In this period the number of books printed in Cambridge but not at the University Press greatly increases, and it is not always possible to distinguish the productions of the University Printers. The attempt is made, but the list does not pretend to be final.

Any additions or corrections to the list will be welcomed. Information and enquiries should be addressed to the ASSISTANT SECRETARY, THE UNIVERSITY PRESS, CAMBRIDGE.

G. R. BARNES

July 1935

UNIVERSITY PRINTERS
1521–1800

Only those names are given which appear in the imprints
of known books

1521.	JOHN SIBERCH	1521–2
1583.	THOMAS THOMAS	D. 1588
1588.	JOHN LEGATE	D. 1620
1606.	CANTRELL LEGGE	D. 1625
1622.	LEONARD GREENE	D. 1630
1625.	THOMAS BUCK, M.A.	At least till 1668
	JOHN BUCK, M.A.	At least till 1668
1630.	FRANCIS BUCK	Resigned 1632
1632.	ROGER DANIEL	Patent cancelled 1650
1650.	JOHN LEGATE (*the younger*)	Patent cancelled 1655
1655.	JOHN FIELD	D. 1668
1669.	JOHN HAYES	D. 1705
1705.	CORNELIUS CROWNFIELD	Pensioned 1740
1730.	WILLIAM FENNER ⎫	
	MARY FENNER ⎪	Lease relinquished by
	THOMAS JAMES ⎬	Mrs Fenner 1738
	JOHN JAMES ⎭	
1740.	JOSEPH BENTHAM	Resigned 1766
1758.	JOHN BASKERVILLE	Nothing after 1763
1766.	JOHN ARCHDEACON	D. 1795
1793.	JOHN BURGES	D. 1802

CAMBRIDGE BOOKS
1521–1800
There is some doubt about the books printed in italics

1521
Bullock (H.). Oratio. 4º.
S. Augustine. De miseria vitae. 4º.
Lucianus. περὶ διψάδων (trans. H. Bullock). 4º.
Baldwin. De Altaris sacramento. 4º.
Erasmus (D.). De conscribendis epistolis. 4º.
Galen (C.). De Temperamentis. Trans. T. Linacre. 4º.
Fisher (J.). Contio. Latin by R. Pace. 4º.

1522
Geminus (Papyrius). Hermathena. 4º.

? 1522
[Lily, W.]. De octo orationis partium constructione libellus. 4º.

1584
Bright (T.). In physicam G. A. Scribonii animadversiones. 8º.
Martinus (J.). De prima corporum generatione. 8º.
Ovidius. Fabularum interpretatio a G. Sabino. [Ed. T. T.]. 8º.
Ramus (P.). Dialecticae libri duo, scholiis G. Tempelli. 8º.
Rouspeau (Yves) and J. de l'Espine. Two treatises, translated. 8º.
Sadeel (A.). [La Roche de Chandieu.] Disputationes. 4º.

1585
Pilkington (Jas.) and Rob. Some. Exposition on Nehemiah etc. 8º.
     ”   ”   Two treatises on Oppression. 8º.
Ramus (P.). Latin Grammar, in English. 8º.
Ursinus (Z.). Doctrinae christianae compendium. 8º.
Whitaker (W.). Answer to a book by W. Rainolds. 2 issues. 8º.
Willet (Andr.). De animae natura et viribus. 8º.

1586
Harmony of Confessions. 8º.
Treatise against the Defense of the Censure. With 2 Treatises by W. Fulke. 8º.

1587
Carmichael (Jas.). Grammaticae Latinae liber II. 4º.
Plato. Menexenus. 4º.
Thomas (Tho.). Dictionarium linguae Latinae. 8º.
Ursinus (Zach.). Explicationes catecheticae. Ed. 2. 8º.

1588

Whitaker (W.). Disputatio de sacra scriptura. 4º.

Achilles Tatius. De Clitophontis et Leucippes amoribus. 8º.
Bastingius (J.). Exposition upon the Catechism. 8º.
Beza (T.). Job expounded. 8º. (n.d.)
„   Ecclesiastes. 8º. (n.d.)
New Testament. (Genevan Version.) 24º.
Willet (Andr.). Sacrorum emblematum centuria una. 4º.

1589

Bastingius (J.). Exposition upon the Catechism. 4º.
Cicero. De oratore libri tres. 16º.
Terentius. Comoediae sex. 12º.
Thomas (Tho.). Dictionarium linguae Latinae. Ed. 2. 8º.

1590

Greenwood (John). Syntaxis et prosodia. 8º.
Holland (Hen.). Treatise against Witchcraft. 4º.
Perkins (Wm.). Armilla Aurea. Ed. 1. 8º.
Whitaker (W.). Answer to a book by W. Rainolds. 8º.
Willet (Andr.). De generali Judaeorum vocatione. 4º.

1591

Bible (Genevan version). 8º.
Perkins (W.). A Golden Chaine. 8º.
„   Armilla Aurea. Ed. 2. 8º.

1592

Bastingius (J.). Exposition upon the Catechism. 8º.
L'Espine (Jean de). A very excellent Discourse (trans. E. Smyth). 4º.
Lipsius (Justus). Tractatus ad historiam Romanam. 8º.
Perkins (W.). Prophetica. 8º.
„   Armilla Aurea. Ed. 3.
„   A Golden Chaine. Ed. 2. 8º.
Sohn (Georg). A briefe and learned Treatise (trans. N. G.). 8º.
Thomas (Tho.). Dictionarium. Ed. 3. 4º.
Zanchius (H.). Spirituall mariage. 16º.

1593

Bell (Thomas). T. Bels Motives. 4º.
[Cowell (John).] Antisanderus. Edd. 1 and 2. 4º.
Fletcher (G.). Poemes of love. 4º.
Lysias. Eratosthenes, praelectionibus illustrata A. Dunaei. 8º.
More (John). Table from the beginning of the world. 8º.
Perkins (W.). Direction for the government of the Tongue. 8º.
„   Two Treatises. 8º.
Thomas (T.). Dictionarium. Ed. 4. 8º.

1594

Danaeus (Lamb.). Commentarie upon the twelve small Prophets. 4⁰.
G[reaves] (P.). Grammatica anglicana. 8⁰.
Hawenreuter (J. L.). Σύνοψις τῆς φυσικῆς τοῦ 'Αριστοτέλους. 8⁰.
The Death of Usury. 4⁰.
Thomas (Tho.). Dictionarium. Ed. 4. 8⁰.
Whitaker (W.). Adv. T. Stapletoni defensionem duplicatio. F⁰.

1595

Bastingius (J.). Exposition upon the Catechism. 8⁰.
C[ovell] (W.). Polimanteia. 2 issues. 4⁰.
Lycophron. 'Αλεξάνδρα. 12⁰.
Perkins (W.). Two Treatises. Ed. 2. 2 edd., 4⁰ and 8⁰.
    ,,   Exposition of the Creed. 4⁰.
    ,,   A Salve for a Sicke man. 8⁰.
    ,,   A Golden Chaine (trans. R. H.). Ed. 2. 4⁰.
    ,,   A Direction for the government of the Tongue. 4⁰.
Plutarchus. Περὶ τοῦ ἀκούειν. 8⁰.
R[acster] [J.]. De hypocritis vitandis. 4⁰.

1596

Du Jon (F.). The Apocalypse (trans. T. Barbar). 4⁰.
G[ibbon] (C.). A Watchworde for Warre. 4⁰.
Perkins (W.). A Declaration...of Christ crucified. 16⁰.
    ,,   A Discourse of Conscience. 8⁰.
    ,,   Exposition of the Creed. Ed. 2. 4⁰.
Some (R.). Three questions. 2 edd. 8⁰.
Thomas (Tho.). Dictionarium. Ed. 5. 4⁰.

1597

Pacius (Julius). Institutiones Logicae. 18⁰.
Perkins (W.). A Declaration...of Christ crucified. 4⁰.
    ,,   A Golden Chaine. Ed. 2. 4⁰.
    ,,   Exposition of the Creede. 8⁰.
    ,,   Salve for a Sicke man (and other tracts). 4⁰.
    ,,   Two Treatises. Ed. 2. 4⁰.
Praecepta in monte Sinai data. (Latine) per Ph. Ferd. Polonum. 4⁰.
Spiritual epistles. 4⁰.

1598

Bird (S.). Lectures upon Hebr. xi and Ps. xxxviii. 8⁰.
    ,,   Lectures upon 2 Cor. viii and ix. 8⁰.
Chemnitius (Mart.). Exposition of the Lords Prayer. 8⁰.
F[letcher], I. Causes of urine. 8⁰.
Lincoln Visitation Articles. 4⁰.
Perkins (W.). De Praedestinationis modo. 8⁰.
    ,,   A Reformed Catholike. 8⁰.
    ,,   Specimen Digesti sive Harmoniae etc. F⁰.
Stoughton (Tho.). General Treatise against Popery. 8⁰.
Terence in English, by R. B[ernard]. 4⁰.
Wilcox (Tho.). Discourse touching the Doctrine of Doubting. 8⁰.

1599

Dillingham (Fra.). A Disswasive from Poperie. 8°.
Polanus (Amandus). Treatise concerning Predestination. 8°.
Whitaker (W.). Praelectiones.+Cygnea Cantio. 4°.
Zanchius (Hieron.). Confession of Christian religion. 8°.

1600

Perkins (W.). A Golden Chaine (and 12 other works). 4°.
Thomas (T.). Dictionarium. Ed. 6. 8°.
Whitaker (W.). Praelectiones de conciliis. 8°.
    ,,   Tractatus de peccato originali. 8°.

1601

An Ease for Overseers of the Poor. 4°.
Hill (Rob.). Life everlasting. 4°.
Perkins (W.). How to live and that well. 12°.
    ,,   A warning against the Idolatry etc. 8°.
[,,   ]The True Gaine. 8°.

1602

Cicero. Epistolae. 8°.
Cogan (Tho.). Epistolarum Ciceronis epitome. 8°.
Dillingham (Fra.). Disputationes adv. R. Bellarminum. 8°.
Pagit (Eusebius). The Historie of the Bible. 12°.
[Perkins (W.).] Treatise of Gods free grace and mans free will. 8°.
Willet (A.). A Catholicon on Jude. 8°.

1603

Dillingham (Fra.). A Quartron of reasons prooved a quartron of follies. 4°.
    ,,   Tractatus in quo ex Papistarum confessione etc. 8°.
Heydon (Sir Christ.). Defence of Judiciall Astrologie. 4°.
James I. A Princes Looking Glasse (trans. W. Willymat). 4°.
Perkins (W.). Works in one volume. F°.
    ,,   A Direction for the Tongue. 12°.
    ,,   A Treatise of the Vocations. 8°.
    ,,   A Treatise of Christian Equitie. 8°.
Playfere (Tho.). Power of Praier. 8°.
    ,,   Heart's delight. 8°.
Sharpe (Leonell). Sermon before the University, 28 March. 8°.
    ,,   Dialogus inter Angliam et Scotiam. 8°.
Smith (J.). The bright morning star. 12°.
Sorrowes Joy. 4°.
Threnothriambeuticon. 4°.
Willet (A.). Ecclesia triumphans. 8°.

1604

Bownde (Nich.). The Holy Exercise of Fasting. 8°.
Gibbon (Cha.). The Order of Equalitie. 4°.
Lincoln Visitation Articles. 4°.
Manning (Jas.). A New Booke intituled I am for you all. 4°.

Oliver (Tho.). De sophismatum praestigiis cavendis. 4⁰.
Perkins (W.). Problema de Romanae fidei ementito catholicismo. 4⁰.
　　　”　　　Commentarie on Galatians. 4⁰.
　　　”　　　First Part of the Cases of Conscience. 8⁰.
　　　”　　　Treatise of Christian Equitie. 8⁰.
　　　”　　　A reformed Catholike. 8⁰.
Willet (A.). Thesaurus ecclesiae. 8⁰.

1605

Bell (Thomas). T. Bels Motives. Ed. 2. 4⁰.
Cowell (John). Institutiones juris Anglicani. 8⁰.
Dillingham (Fra.). Spicilegium de Antichristo. 8⁰.
　　　”　　　Sermon. 8⁰.
In homines nefarios. (Gunpowder Plot.) 4⁰.
Leech (J.). Plaine and Profitable Catechisme for Householders. 8⁰.
Perkins (W.). Works. Vol. 1. F⁰.
Playfere (Tho.). The Sick Man's Couch. 8⁰.
Willet (A.). Hexapla in Genesin. F⁰.

1606

A Supplication of the Family of Love examined. 4⁰.
Dillingham (Fra.). Disputatio de natura Poenitentiae. 8⁰.
　　　”　　　Progresse in Pietie. 8⁰.
Hieron (Sam.). Truths Purchase. 8⁰.
Perkins (W.). Cases of Conscience. 8⁰.
Thomas (T.). Dictionarium. Ed. 7. 4⁰.

1607

Bernard (R.). A Double Catechisme. 8⁰.
　　　”　　　Terence. Ed. 2. 4⁰.
Cowell (John). The Interpreter. 4⁰.
Hieron (Sam.). Three Sermons. 4⁰.
　　　”　　　The Dignity of the Scripture. 4⁰.
Lipsius (Just.). Tractatus ad historiam Rom. cognoscendam. 8⁰.
Perkins (W.). A Treatise of Man's Imagination. 12⁰.
[Rogers (Tho.).] The Faith of the Church of England. 4⁰.
Walsall (Sam.). Sermon before the King at Royston. 4⁰.
Willet (A.). Loidoromastix. 4⁰.
　　　”　　　Harmonie upon Samuel i. 4⁰.

1608

Bownde (N.). Unbeleefe of S. Thomas. Treatise of Consolation. 8⁰.
Hieron (S.). Sixe sermons. 4⁰.
Kilby (R.). The burthen of a loaden conscience. 8⁰.
Perkins (W.). A discourse of the damned art of witchcraft. 8⁰.
　　　”　　　The foundation of Christian religion. 8⁰.
　　　”　　　The whole treatise of the Cases of Conscience. 8⁰.
　　　”　　　A godly exposition of Christs Sermon in the Mount. 4⁰.
　　　”　　　Works. Vol. 1. F⁰.
Walkington (T.). Salomons sweet harpe. 8⁰.

1609

Bernard (R.). A double Catechisme. 8⁰.
Hieron (S.). Three sermons: A Remedie for securitie etc. 4⁰.
Perkins (W.). Works. Vol. II. [Iohn Legat.] F⁰.
    ,,   Works. Vol. III. [Cantrell Legge.] F⁰.
Playfere (T.). [Four Sermons.] 4⁰.

1610

Anthonie (Fr.). Medicinae, chymicae, et veri potabilis auri assertio, etc. 4⁰.
Ely Visitation Articles. 4⁰.
Fletcher (Giles). Christs Victorie. 4⁰.
Owen (D.). Herod and Pilate reconciled. 4⁰.
Perkins (W.). A discourse of the damned art of witchcraft. Ed. 2. 8⁰.
Playfere (T.). Ten sermons. 8⁰.
Thomas (T.). Dictionarium. Ed. 8. 8⁰.
Willet (A.). Hexapla in Danielem. F⁰.

1611

Perkins (W.). A godly exposition of Christs Sermon in the Mount. 4⁰.
Playfere (T.). Power of Praier. 8⁰.
    ,,   The Sick Man's Couch. 8⁰.
Willet (A.). Hexapla upon Romans. F⁰.

1612

Cambridge University Act Verses.
Collins (S.). Increpatio Andreae Eudaemono-Johannis Jesuitae. 4⁰.
Epicedium Cantabrigiense. 2 edd. 4⁰.
Nethersole (Sir F.). Laudatio funebris. 4⁰.
Perkins (W.). A Golden Chaine. Ed. 2. 8⁰.
Playfere (T.). Nine sermons. 8⁰.
Pownoll (N.). The young divines apologie. 8⁰.
Taylor (T.). Commentarie upon the epistle of Paul to Titus. 4⁰.
    ,,   Japhets first publique perswasion into Sems tents. 4⁰.

1613

Despotinus (Gaspar). Hirci Mulctra disceptatio medica. 4⁰.
Perkins (W.). Works. Vol. III. F⁰.
Robartes (Foulke). The Revenue of the Gospel is tythes. 4⁰.

1614

Ely Visitation Articles. 4⁰.
Kilby (R.). The Burthen. Ed. 5. 8⁰.
Mosse (Miles). Justifying and Saving Faith distinguished. 4⁰.
Willet (Andr.). Harmonie upon the first booke of Samuel. F⁰.
    ,,   Harmonie upon the second booke of Samuel. F⁰.
    ,,   Ecclesia Triumphans. 3 pts. F⁰.

1615

[? Brooke, S.] Melanthe. Fabula Pastoralis. 4⁰.
God and the King, a dialogue. 8⁰.
Yates (John). God's arraignment of Hypocrites. 4⁰.

1616

Farley (Henry). The Complaint of Paules to all Christian soules. 4⁰.
Gostwyke (Roger). The Anatomie of Ananias. 4⁰.
James I. Remonstrance for the Right of Kings. 4⁰.
Kilby (R.). The Burthen. Ed. 6. 12⁰.
Office of Christian parents. 4⁰.
Stirbridge Fair Passes.
Yates (J.). God's arraignment. 4⁰.

1617

Collins (Sam.). Epphata to F. T. 4⁰.
Hieron (Sam.). David's Penitential Psalm opened in 30 several lectures. 4⁰.

1618

Kilby (R.). Hallelu-iah. 8⁰.
    „   The Burthen. Ed. 7. 8⁰.
Perkins (W.). Works. Vol. III. F⁰.
Taylor (Tho.). Christ's Combate and Conquest. 4⁰.

1619

Angelos (Christopher). Ἐγκώμιον Μεγάλης Βρεττανίας. 4⁰.
    „   Ἐγχειρίδιον, Περὶ τῆς καταστάσεως τῶν Ἑλλήνων. 4⁰.
Gurnay (Edm.). Corpus Christi, a sermon. 12⁰.
James I. Remonstrance for the Right of Kings. 2 eds. 4⁰.
Lacrymae Cantabrigienses in obitum Annae. 4⁰.
Norwich Visitation Articles. 4⁰.
Sympson (W.). Full and profitable interpretation of proper names. 4⁰.
Taylor (Tho.). Commentarie upon the Epistle to Titus. 4⁰.

1620

Willet (Andr.). Hexapla upon Romans. F⁰.

1621

[Lily (W.).] Short Introduction of Grammar. 8⁰.
Playfere (Tho.). Nine Sermons. 8⁰.

1622

Owen (David). Anti-Paraeus. 8⁰.

1623

Crakanthorpe (Ric.). De providentia Dei. 4⁰.
Gratulatio de S. P. reditu ex Hispaniis. (2 states.) 4⁰.
Herbert (G.). Oratio de Principis Caroli reditu ex Hispaniis. 4⁰.
The Whole Booke of Psalmes with apt notes to sing them. 8⁰.

1624

Chevalier (Guillaume de). The Ghosts of the deceased Sieurs de Villemor. 8⁰.
Sudbury Visitation Articles. 4⁰.

1625

Almanack. (Sheet c only.) 8°.
Cantabrigiensium Dolor et Solamen. 4°.
      ,,   (with additions). 4°.
Epithalamium Caroli Regis et H. Mariae Reginae. 4°.

1626

Almanack (Strof). 8°.
Benlowes (E.). Sphinx theologica. 8°.
Holland (Abr.). Hollandi Post-huma. 4°.
Nowell (A.). Christianae pietatis prima institutio. 8°.
Sarpi (Paolo). Interdicti Veneti historia (trans. into Latin, W. Bedell). 4°.

1627

Almanacks (Dove, Frost, Lakes, Rivers, Strof, Waters). 8°.
Davenant (Joh.). Expositio epistolae ad Colossenses. F°.
Fletcher (Phineas). Locustae. 4°.
Lincoln Visitation Articles. 4°.
Mede (Jos.). Clavis Apocalyptica. 4°.
Perrot (Rich.). Jacob's Vowe, or the true historie of Tithes. 4°.
Sudbury Visitation Articles. 4°.
Ward (W.). Grounds of Catechisme. 8°.
Winterton (R.). Gerhard. Meditations. 12°.
Wren (Matth.). Sermon before the Kings Majestie. 4°.

1628

Bedell (Wm.). Examination of certaine motives to Recusansie. 8°.
Carter (John). Winter evenings communication with young novices. 8°.
Dent (Daniel). Sermon against drunkenness. 4°.
New Testament. 24°.
Psalms in metre. 8° and 12°.

1629

Almanacks (Clarke, Pond, Rivers). 8°.
Bible. F°.
Common Prayer. F°.
Psalms in metre. F°.

1630

Almanack (Rivers). 8°.
Bible. B. L. 4°.
     ,,   Roman Letter. 4°.
Cicero de Officiis etc. 8°.
Common Prayer. 4°.
Davenant (John). Expositio epistolae ad Colossenses. Ed. 2. F°.
Lincoln Visitation Articles. 4°.
Pemble (W.). De Formarum Origine. 16°.
Psalms in metre. 4°.
[Sarpi (Paolo).] Quaestio quodlibetica (trans. W. Bedell). 4°.

1631

Almanack (Kidman). 8°.
Aphthonius. Progymnasmata. 8°.
Castalio (Seb.). Dialogorum sacrorum libri IV. 8°.

Cicero. Epistolarum libri VI, a Jo. Sturmio. 8⁰.
Davenant (Jo.). Praelectiones. F⁰.
Genethliacum Caroli et Mariae. 4⁰.
Hippocratis aphorismorum liber primus, Gr. et Lat. 4⁰.
Moses Maimonides. Canones poenitentiae, Latine a G. N. 4⁰.
Ovidius. Metamorphoses. 12⁰.
Seton (J.). Dialectica. 8⁰.
Talaeus (Aud.). Rhetorica. 8⁰.
Winterton (R.). Gerhard. Meditations, Ed. 2.+Prayers, Ed. 3. 12⁰.

1632

Anthologia in Regis Exanthemata. 4⁰.
Cruso (John). Militarie instructions for the Cavallerie. F⁰.
Dalechamp (Caleb). Christian Hospitalitie. Harrisonus honoratus. 4⁰.
Fletcher (Giles). Christs Victorie. Ed. 2. 4⁰.
Heywood (Tho.). Englands Elisabeth. 12⁰.
Mede (Jos.). Clavis apocalyptica. Ed. 2. 4⁰.
Novum Testamentum, graece. 8⁰.
Randolph (Tho.). The Jealous Lovers. (2 states.) 4⁰.
Schonaeus (Corn.). Terentius Christianus. 8⁰.
Spagnuoli (B.). B. Mantuani Adolescentia. 8⁰.
Vergil. Opera. 8⁰.
Winterton (R.). Gerhard. A Golden Chaine. 12⁰.
    „   „   Meditations, Ed. 3.+Prayers, Ed. 4. 12⁰.

1633

Bible. (2 states.) 4⁰.
Castalio (Seb.). Dialogorum sacrorum libri IV. 8⁰.
Cicero de Officiis etc. 12⁰.
Corderius (Matth.). Colloquiorum scholasticorum libri IV. 8⁰.
Ducis Eboracensis fasciae a Musis Cantabrig. raptim contextae. 4⁰.
Fletcher (Giles). De literis antiquae Britanniae etc. 8⁰.
Fletcher (Phineas). The Purple Island, etc. 4⁰.
F[letcher] (P)[hineas]. Sylva Poetica. 8⁰.
Fosbrooke (Joh.). Six sermons [and separately]. 4⁰.
Hausted (Peter). Senile Odium, comoedia. 8⁰.
Herbert (George). The Temple. (2 states.) 12⁰.
    „   „   Ed. 2. 12⁰.
Hippocrates. Aphorismi, graece.+Epigrammata Reg. Med. Professorum. 8⁰.
Kellet (Edw.). Miscellanies of Divinitie. F⁰.
Morton (T.). Broadsheet.
New Testament. 4⁰.
Norwich Visitation Articles. 4⁰.
Nowell (Alex.). Christianae pietatis prima institutio. 8⁰.
Peterborough Visitation Articles. 𝕭. 𝕷. 4⁰.
Psalms with apt notes. 𝕭. 𝕷. 4⁰.
Rex redux. 4⁰.
Scot (Tho.). Assize Sermon at Bury St Edmunds. 4⁰.
Scott (J.). Broadsheet containing list of officers etc. (Fragments.)
The Christian's Race. 4⁰.
Vives (Joan. Lud.). Linguae Latinae exercitatio. 8⁰.
Winterton (R.). Dionysius de situ orbis. 8⁰.

1634

Almanacks (Clark, Dove, Kidman, Rivers, Swallow, Turner, Winter). 8⁰.
Cantebrigia (*Map*).
Crashaw (R.). Epigrammatum sacrorum liber. 8⁰.
Davenant (John). Determinationes quaestionum theologicarum. F⁰.
Donne (John). Six sermons [and 1 and 6 separately]. 4⁰.
Erasmus. Epitome colloquiorum. 8⁰.
Foundation of the University. Broadsheet.
Garthwaite (H.). Μονοτέσσαρον. The Evangelicall Harmonie. 4⁰.
Gerhard (John). Meditationes Sacrae. 24⁰.
Golius (Theophilus). Epitome doctrinae moralis ex decem libris Aristotelis. 8⁰.
Hawkins (Will.). Corolla varia. Eclogae Virgilianae. 8⁰.
Herbert (Geo.). The Temple. Ed. 3. 12⁰.
Lessius (Leonardus). Hygiasticon, Cornaro's Treatise. Edd. 1 and 2. 12⁰.
[Lily (Wm.).] A short introduction of Grammar. 8⁰.
Psalms in metre. 4⁰.
Randolph (Thos.). The Jealous Lovers. 4⁰.
Russell (John). The two famous pitcht battles of Lypsich and Lutzen. 4⁰.
Spagnuoli (B.). B. Mantuani adolescentia. 8⁰.

1635

Aesopus, Fabulae. 8⁰.
Almanack (Kidman).
Aphthonius. Progymnasmata. 8⁰.
Bible. 4⁰.
  „ 𝕭. 𝕷. 4⁰.
Carmen natalitium ad cunas principis Elizabethae. 4⁰.
Common Prayer. 4⁰.
Cuique suum. Ἀντῳδὴ contra Cathari cantilenam. 4⁰.
Herbert (Geo.). The Temple. Ed. 4. 12⁰.
Kellet (Edw.). Miscellanies of Divinitie. F⁰.
Lincoln Visitation Articles. 4⁰.
Ovidius. Heroides, Amores, De arte amandi. 8⁰.
Ravisius (Joannes). Epistolae. 16⁰.
Schonaeus (Corn.). Terentius Christianus. 8⁰.
Shelford (Rob.). Five pious and learned discourses. 4⁰.
Spagnuoli (B.). B. Mantuani adolescentia. 8⁰.
Swan (John). Speculum mundi. 4⁰.
Talaeus (Aud.). Rhetorica. 12⁰.
Winterton (R.). Poetae minores Graeci. 8⁰.
  „   Gerhard. Meditations, Ed. 4.+Prayers, Ed. 5. 12⁰.

1636

Almanack (Dove).
Benlowes (Ed.). Sphinx Theologica. 8⁰.
Cade (Ant.). Sermon on Conscience. Appendix. 4⁰.
Dalechamp (C.). Haeresologia Tripartita. 4⁰.
Dugres (Gabriel). Grammaticae Gallicae compendium. 8⁰.
Hodson (William). Credo resurrectionem carnis. Ed. 2. 12⁰.
Lessius (Leonardus). Hygiasticon. Ed. 3. 12⁰.

Manutius (Aldus). Phrases linguae Latinae. 8⁰.
[Nowell (Alex.).] Christianae pietatis prima institutio. 8⁰.
Saltmarsh (John). Poemata sacra, latine et anglice scripta. 8⁰.
Simson (Edw.). Mosaica. 4⁰.
Winterton (R.). Drexelius, Considerations upon Eternitie. 12⁰.

1637

Bible. (Colophon 1638.) 4⁰.
  „ 𝕭. 𝕷. 4⁰.
  „   8⁰.
Burgersdicius (Fr.). Institutiones Logicae. 8⁰.
Common Prayer. F⁰ and 8⁰.
D[uport] (J.). Θρηνοθρίαμβος, seu liber Job graeco carmine. 8⁰.
Morton (Tho.). Antidotum. 4⁰.
Peterborough Visitation Articles. 4⁰.
Psalms in metre. 𝕭. 𝕷. 4⁰.
  „   Roman Letter. 4⁰.
Συνῳδία sive Musarum Cantabrigiensium concentus. 4⁰.

1638

Almanacks (Dove, Rivers, Swallow, Winter).
Bible. F⁰ and 4⁰.
Common Prayer. F⁰, 4⁰ and 8⁰.
Directions for musters. 4⁰.
Herbert (Geo.). The Temple. Ed. 5. 12⁰.
Isocrates. Orationes et Plutarchus. 8⁰.
Justa Edouardo King...+Obsequies. 4⁰.
Norwich Visitation Articles. 4⁰.
Ovidius. De tristibus. 8⁰.
Psalms in metre. F⁰ and 4⁰.
Sictor, J. Panegyricon inaugurale Praetoris Regii. 4⁰.
Winterton (R.). Gerhard. Meditations, Ed. 5.+Prayers, Ed. 6. 12⁰.

1639

Almanack (Swallow). 8⁰.
Bible. 𝕭. 𝕷. 4⁰.
Cade (Anthony). Sermon on Conscience. Appendix. 4⁰.
Cicero de Officiis etc. 8⁰.
Davenant (Jo.). Expositio epistolae ad Colossenses. Ed. 3. F⁰.
  „   Determinationes.... Ed. 2. F⁰.
Du Praissac (Sieur). Military Discourses. Englished by J. C[ruso]. 8⁰.
  „   Arte of Warre, etc. 8⁰.
Fuller (Tho.). The Historie of the Holie Warre. F⁰.
Gurnay (Edm.). Towards the vindication of the Second Commandment. 24⁰
H[odson] (W.). The Holy Sinner. 12⁰.
Morton (T.). Antidotum. 4⁰.
Peterborough Visitation Articles. 4⁰.
Psalms in metre. 𝕭. 𝕷. 4⁰.
Sudbury Visitation Articles. 4⁰.
Winterton (R.). Drexelius, Considerations upon Eternitie. 12⁰.

1640

Almanacks (Rivers, Swallow). 8⁰.
Ball (J.). A friendly trial of the grounds tending to Separation. (2 states.) 4⁰.
B[enlowes] (E.). A Buckler against the fear of death. 8⁰.
Bible. 𝕭. 𝕷. 4⁰. (N.T. title 1639.)
Common Prayer. 𝕭. 𝕷. 4⁰.
Davenant (J.). Ad fraternam communionem adhortatio. 12⁰.
Downame (G.). A Godly and learned treatise of Prayer. 4⁰.
Drexelius (H.). The School of Patience. 12⁰.
Endeavour of making the principles of the Christian religion plain. 8⁰.
Eustachius (Fr.). Summa philosophiae quadripartita. 8⁰.
Fenner (W.). The Souls Looking-glasse. 8⁰.
Fletcher (Giles). Christs Victory. 4⁰.
Fuller (Tho.). Historie of the Holy Warre. Ed. 2. F⁰.
Gerhard (Joh.). The Summe of Christian Doctrine. 24⁰.
Gower (J.). Ovids Festivalls. 8⁰.
Heinsius (Dan.). Sacrarum exercitationum libri xx. Ed. 2. 4⁰.
H[odson] (W.). The Divine Cosmographer. 12⁰.
[Lily (W.).] A short introduction of grammar. 8⁰.
Morton (Tho.). Decisio controversiae de eucharistia. 4⁰.
Posselius (Joh.). Syntaxis graeca. 8⁰.
Ramus (P.). Dialecticae libri duo. 12⁰.
Randolph (T.). The Jealous Lovers. 8⁰.
Rohan (Henri de). The Complete Captain: trans. J[ohn] C[ruso]. 8⁰.
Torriano (G.). Directions for the Italian Tongue. 4⁰ (n.d.).
Voces votivae. 4⁰.
Winterton (R.). Gerhard. Meditations, Ed. 6.+Prayers, Ed. 7. 12⁰.

1641

Andrewes (Lancelot). Nineteen sermons concerning Prayer. 12⁰.
Christian's Pattern, The. 12⁰.
Davenant (John). Animadversions upon a treatise (of S. Hoard). 8⁰.
Dury (J.). On Peace ecclesiastical. 4⁰.
Gataker (T.). Defence of Anthony Wotton. 8⁰.
Herbert (G.). The Temple. Ed. 6. 12⁰.
Heywood (T.). England's Elisabeth. 12⁰.
Irenodia Cantabrigiensis. 4⁰.
Layer (John). Office and Duty of Constables. 8⁰.
L'Estrange (Hamon). Gods Sabbath etc. 4⁰.
Maisterson (Henr.). Sermon on Hebr. xiii. 18. 4⁰.
Manuell, A, or a Justice of Peace his Vade-mecum. 12⁰.
Munning (Humphry). A Pious Sermon etc. 4⁰.
Psalms in metre. 12⁰.
Salernitanus, B. De Fontibus Artium. 12⁰.
Sherman (J.). A Greek in the Temple. 4⁰.
Thorndike (H.). Of the Government of Churches, a Discourse etc. 8⁰.
Warme Beere, or, A Treatise. 12⁰.

1642

Almanacks (Dove, Swallow). 8⁰.
Demosthenes. Orationes Selectae. Gr. et Lat. 12⁰.

Du Praissac (Sieur). Military Discourses. Englished by J. C[ruso]. 8⁰.
Fern (Henry). Resolving of Conscience. (3 states.) 4⁰.
Fuller (Tho.). The Holy State. F⁰.
His Majesty's Declaration to all His loving Subjects. Aug. 12, 1642. 4⁰.
    „   Answer to Declaration of Parliament of July 1. 4⁰.
Holdsworth (Ri.). Sermon in St Maries upon Mar. 27. 4⁰.
Kempis (T.). Of the following of Christ. 8⁰.
Love (Ri.). The Watchman's Watchword. 4⁰.
Magirus (Jo.). Physiologicae Peripateticae libri VI. 8⁰.
More (Hen.). Ψυχωδία Platonica. (2 states.) 8⁰.
Novum Testamentum (Beza). (2 states.) F⁰.
Petition of the Commons of Kent. 4⁰.
Petition of Lords and Commons, and His Majestie's Answer. 4⁰.
Proclamation. Forbidding all Levies of Forces. Broadsheet.
Proclamation. That no Popish Recusant shall serve. 4⁰.
[Spelman (Sir J.).] A Protestant's Account of his Orthodox Holding. 4⁰.
Thorndike (Herbert). Of Religious Assemblies. 8⁰.
Torriano (G.). Select Italian Proverbs. 12⁰.
Watson (Ri.). Sermon touching Schisme. 4⁰.
Wollebius (J.). Compendium Theologiae Christianae. 12⁰.

1643

Beda. Historia Ecclesiastica. F⁰.
Catalogue of remarkable mercies conferred upon the seven counties. 4⁰.
Fenner (W.). The Souls Looking-Glasse. 8⁰.
Introductio ad Sapientiam. 24⁰.
Jackson (Art.). Help. 4⁰.
Minucius Felix (M.). Octavius. 16⁰.
Quarles (Fra.). Emblemes. Ed. 2. 8⁰.
Revindication of Psalme 105. 5, Touch not mine Anointed. 4⁰.
Swan (John). Speculum Mundi. Ed. 2. 4⁰.

1644

Beda. Historia Ecclesiastica. F⁰. (New title only.)
Burgersdicius (Fra.). Institutiones Logicae. 8⁰.
Crofts (J.). The copy of a letter. 4⁰.
Dering (Sir Edw.). A Discourse of Proper Sacrifice. (2 titles.) 4⁰.
Grimston (Sir H.). A Christian New Years gift. 16⁰.
Lambarde (W.). Ἀρχαιονομία. F⁰.
Totius Rhetoricae adumbratio in usum Paulinae Schol. 8⁰.
Winterton (R.). Gerhard. Meditations, Ed. 7 + Prayers, Ed. 8. 12⁰.

1645

Bible. 12⁰. (*N.T. title* 1646.)
Bythner (Victorinus). Lingua Eruditorum. 8⁰.
Chronometra aliquot memorabilium rerum his certis annis gestarum etc. 4⁰.
Crofts (J.). The copy of a letter. Ed. 2. 4⁰.
Howell (James). Δενδρολογία. Dodona's Grove. Ed. 3. 12⁰. (2 states.)
Psalms in metre. 4⁰.
Sarson (L.). Analysis of 1 Tim. i. 15; Chronologia Vapulans. 4⁰.
Shelton (T.). Tachygraphy. 8⁰.
Stahl (D.). Axiomata Philosophica. 12⁰.

1646

Ames (W.). Philosophemata. 12⁰.
Bible. 8⁰.
Britannicus his blessing (in verse). 4⁰.
Buxtorf (Jo.). Epitome Grammaticae Hebraeae. 8⁰.
Duport (J.). Tres libri Solomonis Graeco carmine. 8⁰.
Hall (John). Poems. 8⁰.
Heinsius (Daniel). Crepundia Siliana. 12⁰.
Jackson (Art.). Annotations. 4⁰.
More (Henry). Democritus Platonissans. 8⁰.
Psalms in metre. 12⁰.
Quarles (F.). Judgment and Mercy for afflicted souls. 8⁰.
Sleidan (J.). De quatuor summis Imperiis libri tres. 24⁰.
Valdesso (John). Divine Considerations. 8⁰.
Winterton (R.) Drexelius, Considerations upon Eternitie. 24⁰.

1647

Animadversions upon proceedings against the XI members. 4⁰.
Bible. 12⁰.
Bolton (Sam.). Fast Sermon. 4⁰.
Burgersdicius (F.). Institutiones Logicae. 8⁰.
Cudworth (R.). Sermon before the House of Commons. 4⁰.
Declaration from Sir Thomas Fairfax and his Councell of Warre. 4⁰.
Fuller (Tho.). Historie of the Holie Warre. Ed. 3. F⁰.
Graecae Grammatices compendium...Westm. 8⁰.
Hammond (H.). Five propositions to the Kings Majesty. 4⁰.
H[austed] (P.). πρόσσω καὶ ὀπίσσω. A Sermon at St Maries, 1640. 4⁰.
Heads of a Charge delivered in the name of the Armie.
Heads presented by the Army to the King...June 19.
Introductio ad Sapientiam. 24⁰.
J. (H.). Modell of a Christian Society.+ Right hand of Christian love. 8⁰.
Letter from the Court at Oatelands. 4⁰.
Manifesto from Sir T. Fairfax June 27. 4⁰.
More (Henry). Philosophicall Poems. 8⁰.
Papers of Intelligence from Cambridge. 4⁰.
Proclamation by his Excellency Sir Thomas Fairfax. 4⁰.
Representation from Sir Tho. Fairfax. 4⁰.
Shelton (T.). Tachygraphy. 8⁰.
Short introduction to Grammar...Westminster. 8⁰.
Solemn Ingagement. 4⁰.
Stierius (Joh.). Praecepta doctrinae tabellis compacta. Ed. noua. 4⁰.
The Kings majesties declaration and profession.
Two petitions of the Counties of Buckingham and Hertford. 4⁰.
Vigerius (Fra.). De praecipuis Gr. dictionis idiotismis. 8⁰.

1648

Anacreon. Odae, Gr. Lat. (ab H. Stephano). 8⁰.
Bible. 12⁰. (6 eds.)
Bythner (Victorinus). Clavis Linguae Sanctae. 8⁰.
Catechisms (Greek). 12⁰.
Caussin (N.). Christian Diary. 12⁰.

Eustachius (Fr.). Summa philosophiae quadripartita. 8⁰.
Fuller (Tho.). Holy and Profane State. Ed. 2. F⁰.
Hill (Tho.). The best and worst of Paul. 4⁰.
Homerus. Ilias. Gr. et Lat. 8⁰.
New Testament. 12⁰.
Psalms in metre. 8⁰.
Wendelin (M. F.). Admiranda Nili. 4⁰.
    ,,   Contemplationes Physicae. 4⁰.
White (Thos.). The smoak of the botomlesse pit. 8⁰.
Wollebius (J.). Compendium Theologiae Christianae. 12⁰.

1649

Dickson (D.). A Short Explanation of the Ep. of Paul to the Hebrews. 8⁰.
Eustachius. Summa philosophica quadripartita. 8⁰.
Harvey (Wm.). Exercitatio Anatomica de Circulatione Sanguinis. (2 states.)
    12⁰.
Jacchaeus (Gilb.). Summa Philosophiae. 12⁰.
Mede (Jos.). Clavis Apocalyptica ex innatis. 4⁰.
Thorndike (H.). Of the Right of the Church in a Christian State. 8⁰.
Torriano (G.). Select Italian Proverbs. 24⁰.

1650

Burgersdijck (Fra.). Collegium Physicum. Ed. 3. 12⁰.
Davenant (John). Dissertationes duae. F⁰.
Thorndike (Herb.). Two Discourses. 8⁰.
Winterton (R.). Drexelius, Considerations upon Eternitie. 24⁰.

1651

Castalio (S.). Dialogorum sacrorum libri IV. 8⁰.
Coldwell (C.). Regulae morum. Broadsheet.
Culverwell (N.). Spiritual Opticks. 4⁰.
Dillingham (W.). Sir F. Vere, Commentaries of War. F⁰.
Fuller (T.). Historie of the Holie Warre. Ed. 4. F⁰.
[More (H.).] The Second Lash of Alazonomastix. 8⁰.
Stephens (T.). Statius. Sylvae. 8⁰.
    ,,   ,,   Achilleis. 8⁰.

1652

Beza (T.). Novum Testamentum. F⁰.
Gataker (T.). Antonini Meditationes. 4⁰.
Mede (J.). Opuscula Latina ad rem Apocalypticam. 4⁰.
Nicols (T.). A Lapidarie. (2 states.) 4⁰.
Winterton (R.). Poetae minores Graeci. 8⁰.

1653

D[uport] (J.). Θρηνοθρίαμβος, sive liber Job graeco carmine. Ed. 2. 8⁰.
Isocrates. Paraenesis. 12⁰.
Lily (W.). Brevissima Institutio. 8⁰.
Ovid. 8⁰.
Scattergood (A.). Annotationes in Vetus Testamentum. 8⁰.
Smith (T.). Daillé's Apology for the Reformed Churches. 8⁰.

1654

Cambridge Victuallers License (Single leaf).
Dove. Prognostication. 8⁰.
Eustachius. St Paulo: Ethica. 8⁰.
Jacchaeus (T.). Onomasticon Poeticum. 8⁰.
Muretus (A.). Terentius. 8⁰.
Oliva Pacis ad Oliverum. 4⁰.
Smetius. Prosodia. 12⁰.

1655

Barrow (I.). Euclid. 8⁰.
Clark (J.). Two Sermons. 12⁰.
Epictetus. Enchiridion. 8⁰.
Porphyrius. De Abstinentia. 8⁰.
Officium Concionatoris. 4⁰.

1656

Aesopus. Fabulae. 8⁰.
Dillingham (W.). Two Sermons. 4⁰.
[„   ] Confessio fidei. 8⁰.
Muretus (A.). Terentius. 8⁰.

1657

Arrowsmith (J.). Tactica Sacra. 4⁰.
Barrow (I.). Euclidis data succincte demonstrata. 8⁰.
Bible. 8⁰.
    „   (N.T. title 1661.)
Corderius (M.). Colloquia. 8⁰.
Dillingham (W.). Sir F. Vere's Commentaries. F⁰.
Dorislaus (I.). Proelium Nuportanum. F⁰.
New Testament. 8⁰.
Psalms in metre. 2 eds. 8⁰.
Stephanus (H.). Statius, Opera. 8⁰.

1658

Aesopus. Fabulae. 8⁰.
Atwell (G.). The faithfull Surveyor. 4⁰.
Bible. 16⁰.
Corderius (M.). Colloquia. 8⁰.
Frost (J.). Select Sermons. F⁰. (Sep. titles 1657.)
Lightfoot (J.). Horae Hebraicae in Chorographiam. 4⁰.
    „   „   in Evang. Matth. 4⁰.
Musarum Cantabrigiensium Luctus and Gratulatio. 2 eds. 4⁰.
Spencer (W.). Origenis contra Celsum. 4⁰.
Winterton (R.). Drexelius, Considerations upon Eternitie. 12⁰.

1659

Arrowsmith (J.). Armilla Catechetica. 4⁰.
Aylesbury (T.). Diatribae de aeterno decreto. 4⁰.
Bible. F⁰.
Cicero. De Officiis, de Amicitia, de Senectute. 8⁰.
[Dillingham (W.).] Confessio Fidei in Latinum versa. 8⁰.

Ivory (J.). A Continuation.
New Testament. Fº.
University Queries. 4º.

1660

Academiae Cantabrigiensis ΣΩΣΤΡΑ. 2 eds. 4º.
Bible. (N.T. title 1659.) Fº.
Burgersdicius (F.). Institutiones Logicae. 8º.
Cicero de Officiis, de Amicitia etc. 8º.
Common Prayer. Fº.
Dunconus (E.). De Adoratione Dei versus Altare. 12º.
Duport (J.). Evangelicall Politie. 4º.
      „   Homeri Gnomologia. 4º.
Gardiner (S.). De efficacia gratiae convertentis. 4º.
H[acon] (J.). A Review of Mr Horn's Catechisme. 8º.
Love (R.). Oratio post regem reducem. 2 eds. 4º.
[Ray (J.).] Catalogus plantarum circa Cantabrigiam nascentium. (2 states.) 8º.
Smith (T.). The Life and Death of Mr William Moore. 8º.
Spencer (J.). The Righteous Ruler. 4º.

1661

Almanacks (Pond, Swan). 8º.
Bible. 8º.
Colet (J.). A Sermon of Conforming and Reforming. 8º.
Lily (W.). Short Introduction of Grammar. 8º.
New Testament. 8º.
Psalms. 8º.
Psalms in metre. 8º.
Savonarola (H.). The Truth of the Christian Faith. 12º.
Stephens (T.). Three Sermons. 12º.
Threni Cantabrigienses in funere Henrici et Mariae. 4º.
Winterton (R.). Poetae minores Graeci. 8º.

1662

Aesopus. Fabulae. 8º.
Anticlassicus (P.). Vindication of the Inner Temple. 8º.
Atwell (G.). The Faithfull Surveyour. 4º.
Common Prayer. 8º.
Duport (J.). Epithalamia Sacra. 8º.
Epithalamia Cantabrigiensia Caroli II et Catharinae. 4º.
H[acon] (J.). A Vindication of the Review. 8º.
Hyde (E.). The true Catholick's Tenure. 8º.
Muretus (A.). Terentius. 8º.
N[ewman] (S.). Concordance. Fº.
New Testament. 8º.
Psalms. 8º.

1663

Almanacks (Dove, Pond, Swan).
Bible. 4º.
      „   8º. (N.T. title 1662.)
Common Prayer. 4º.
Fortrey (S.). England's Interest. 8º.
Heereboord (A.). Logica (Ἑρμηνεία) seu Synopseos. 8º.

[Kerr (T.).] Ichabod. 4⁰.
Le Franc (J.). The Touchstone of Truth.
Lightfoot (J.). Horae Hebraicae in Evang. Marc. (2 pts.) 4⁰.
Psalms in metre. 4⁰.
[Ray (J.).] Appendix ad Catalogum. 8⁰ and 12⁰.
Spencer (J.). A Discourse concerning Prodigies. 4⁰.
Vossius (G. J.). Elementa Rhetorica.
Winterton (R.). Epigrammata Therapeutica. 8⁰.

1664

Almanacks (Dove, Pond, Swallow, Swan).
Bible. 12⁰.
Homerus. Ilias. 8⁰.
   „   Odyssea. 8⁰.
Psalms (Greek). 12⁰ and 8⁰.
Salmasius (C.). L. Annaeus Florus.
Whear (D.). Methodus legendi historias. 8⁰.

1665

Almanacks (Dove, Pond, Swallow, Swan). 8⁰.
Beaumont (J.). Observations upon the Apologie of Dr Henry More. 4⁰.
Bellum Belgicum Secundum. 4⁰.
Castalio (S.). Biblia Sacra.
Common Prayer (Greek). 12⁰ and 8⁰.
Duhamel (J. B.). Elementa Astronomica. 12⁰.
Edwards (J.). The Plague of the Heart. 4⁰.
Fournier (G.). Euclid. 12⁰.
Hoole (C.). Terminations of Declensions. 8⁰.
New Testament (Greek). 2 eds. 12⁰.
Old Testament (Greek). (2 states.) 12⁰.
Sallustius. 12⁰.
Sophocles. Tragoediae. 8⁰.
Swan (J.). Speculum Mundi. Ed. 3. 4⁰.

1666

Almanacks (Dove, Pond, Swallow, Swan). 8⁰.
Bible. 4⁰.
Burgersdicius (F.). Institutiones Logicae, et Synopsis. 8⁰.
Common Prayer. 4⁰.
Duport (J.). Psalms in Greek verse. 4⁰.
Heereboord (A.). Ἑρμηνεία Logica. Ed. 2. 8⁰.
New Testament. 4⁰.
Pachymerius (G.). Epitome Logices Aristotelis. 8⁰.
Psalms in metre. 4⁰.

1667

Almanacks (Dove, Pond, Swan). 8⁰.
[Bullokar (John).] An English Expositour. 12⁰.
Dillingham (T.). Visitation Articles. 4⁰.
Salmasius (C.). L. Annaeus Florus. 12⁰.
Winterton (R.). Poetae minores Graeci. 8⁰.

1668

Almanacks (Dove, Pond, Swallow). 8⁰.
Bible. 4⁰.
„   (N.T. title 1666.) 4⁰.
Burgersdicius (F.). Institutiones Logicae, et Synopsis. 8⁰.
Concordance. 4⁰.
Galtruchius (P.). Mathematicae totius Institutio. 8⁰.
Hill (J.). Schrevelius, Lexicon. 4⁰.
Jackson (J.). Index Biblicus. 4⁰.
Kemp (E.). University Sermon. 4⁰.
Sophocles. Scholia. 8⁰.
Starkey (W.). The divine obligation of human ordinances. 4⁰.

1669

Aesopus. Fabulae. 8⁰.
Almanacks (Dove, Pond, Swan, Whiting). 8⁰.
Casaubon (M.). Letter to P. du Moulin. 4⁰.
Dictionarium etymologicum. 4⁰.
Ellis (J.). Clavis Fidei. 8⁰.
Gouldman (F.). Dictionary. Ed. 2. 4⁰.
Livius. 8⁰.
Protestant Almanack. 8⁰.
Scargill (D.). Recantation. 4⁰.
Sophocles. Tragoediae. 8⁰.
Spencer (J.). Dissertatio de Urim et Thummim. 8⁰.
Threni Cantabrigienses in exequiis Henriettae Mariae. 4⁰.

1670

Almanacks (Dove, Pond, Swallow, Swan). 8⁰.
Barne (M.). Sermon at Newmarket. 4⁰.
Bible. 4⁰.
Cato. Disticha de moribus cum Scholiis Erasmi. 8⁰.
Common Prayer. 4⁰.
Crashaw (R.). Poemata et Epigrammata. Ed. 2. 8⁰.
„   Steps to the Temple. 8⁰.
Culmann (L.). Sententiae Pueriles. 8⁰.
Dillingham (T.). Visitation Articles. 4⁰.
Gallus (E.). Pueriles Confabulatiunculae. 8⁰.
Heereboord (A.). Logica. Ed. nova. 8⁰.
Hume (J.). Character of a heavenly conversation.
Johnson (J.). The Judges Authority. 4⁰.
„   Nature inverted. 4⁰.
Lacrymae Cantabrigienses in obitum...Henriettae. 4⁰.
Molinaeus (P.). Poematum libelli tres. 8⁰.
New Testament. 4⁰.
Ovid. Tristia. 8⁰.
Psalms in metre. 4⁰.
R[ay] (J.). Collection of Proverbs. 8⁰.
Seignior (G.). Sermon at Saxham. 4⁰.
Sheringham (R.). De Anglorum gentis origine. 8⁰.
Spencer (J.). Dissertatio de Urim et Thummim. Ed. 2. 8⁰.

Sturm (J.). Cicero, Epistolarum Libri IV. 8º.
Threnodia in obitum Georgii Ducis Albaemarlae. 4º.
Winterton (R.). Gerhard, Meditations. 12º.

1671

Almanacks (Dove, Pond, Swallow, Swan). 8º.
B[ullokar] (J.). An English Expositour. 12º.
Epicedia in obitum Principis Annae. 4º.
Gale (T.). Opuscula Mythologica. 8º. (Sep. titles 1670.)
Laney (B.). Ely Visitation Articles. 4º.
Lily (W.). Short Introduction of Grammar. 8º.
North (J.). Sermon before King at Newmarket. (2 eds.) 4º.
Winterton (R.). Poetae minores Graeci. 8º.
„   Drexelius, Considerations. 12º.

1672

Almanacks (Dove, Pond, Swallow, Swan). 8º.
Homer, Iliad.
Ivory (J.). Foundation of the University. Broadsheet.
N[ewman] (S.). Concordance. Ed. 2. Fº.
Ovid. Metamorphoses. 8º.
Pearson (J.). Vindiciae Epistolarum Ignatii (with Vossius, Epistolae). 4º.
Puffendorf (S.). Elementa Jurisprudentiae. 8º.
Ramus (P.). Dialectic. 8º.
Ravisius (J.). Epistolae. 8º.
Schrevelius (C.). Hesiod. 8º.
Sophocles (Greek and Latin). 8º.
Varenius (B.). Geographia Generalis. Ed. Isaac Newton. 8º.

1673

Almanack. 8º.
Barclay (J.). Argenis (engraved title 1674.) 8º.
Bible. 4º.
Catechesis in usum scholae Buriensis. 8º.
Common Prayer. 4º.
Fortrey (S.). England's Interest. Ed. 2. 8º.
Friendly Vindication of Dryden. 4º.
Grotius. De principiis juris naturalis. 8º.
Lily (W.). Short Introduction of Grammar. 8º.
Muretus (A.). Terentius. 16º.
North (J.). Plato, Dialogi Selecti. 8º.
Psalms in metre. 4º.
Smith (J.). Select Discourses. Ed. 2. 4º.
Sophocles, Tragoediae. 8º.
Varenius (B.). Descriptio Japoniae. 8º.

1674

Almanack (Dove). 8º.
Bible. Fº.
Casimir (M.). Lyricorum Libri. 24º.
Cicero. De officiis, etc. 8º.

Crashaw (R.). Poemata et Epigrammata. Ed. 2 (corrected). 8°.
Gouldman (F.). Dictionary. Ed. 3.
Lightfoot (J.). Horae Hebraicae in Evang. Luc. 4°.
Olivier (P.). Dissertationes Academicae. 8°.
Ovid. Heroides. 8°.

1675

Almanack (Swan). 8°.
Bible. 4°.
Common Prayer. 4°.
Faber (T.). Lucretius. De Rerum Natura. 12°.
Ivory (J.). A Continuation.
Jackson (W.). Of the Rule of Faith. 4°.
Magna et antiqua charta Quinque Portuum. 8°.
M[arvell] (A.). Plain Dealing. 12°.
Psalms in Metre. 4°.
[Rogers (T.).] Faith professed in the xxxix Articles. 4°.

1676

Beza (T.). Novum Testamentum. 12°.
Briggs (W.). Ophthalmo-graphia. 8°.
B[ullokar] (J.). An English Expositour. 12°.
Common Prayer. 4°.
D[uport (J.).] Musae Subsecivae. 8°.
Minellius (J.). Terentius. 12°.
Muretus (A.). Terentius. 8°.
North (Sir T.). Plutarch's Lives. F°.
Psalms in metre. 4°.
Rhodokanakis (C.). Tractatus de resolutione verborum. 8°.
Robertson (W.). Thesaurus Graecae Linguae. 4°.
Scattergood (S.). Sermon before the King at Newmarket. 4°.
Simon (M.). Opera Theologica.
Spencer (W.). Origen, Philokalia. 4°.
Templer (J.). Visitation Sermon. 4°.

1677

Beza (T.). Novum Testamentum. 24°.
Bible. 4°.
      „   (N.T. title 1675.)
Epithalamium in nuptiis Gulielmi-Henrici Arausii et Mariae. 4°.
Spencer (W.). Origen, Contra Celsum. 4°.
W[alker] (W.). Plea for Infant Baptism. 8°.
Winterton (R.). Poetae minores Graeci. 8°.
Wittie (R.). Gout Raptures. 4°.

1678

Almanacks (Dove, Pond, Swallow, Swan). 8°.
Babington (H.). Mercy and Judgment. 4°.
Badius (J.). Baptista Mantuanus. 8°.
Gouldman (F.). Dictionary. Ed. 4. 4°.
Ray (J.). English Proverbs. Ed. 2. 8°.

1679

Almanacks (Dove, Pond, Swallow, Swan). 8⁰.
Bible. 4⁰.
Common Prayer. 4⁰.
Crashaw (R.). Poemata et Epigrammata. 8⁰.
Heinsius (D.). Andronicus Rhodius, Ethicorum Paraphrasis. 8⁰.
Homer. Ilias. Ed. postrema. 8⁰.
Livius. Historia. 8⁰.
Psalms in metre. 4⁰.
Sallustius. 12⁰.

1680

Almanacks (Culpepper, Dove, Pond, Swallow, Swan). 8⁰.
B[ullokar] (J.). An English Expositour. 12⁰.
Burgersdicius (F.). Institutiones Logicae. 8⁰.
Florus, Pontanus, Ampelius. 12⁰.
Heereboord (A.). Ἑρμηνεία Logica. Ed. nova. 8⁰.
New Testament. (Engraved table 1683.) 4⁰.

1681

Almanack (Wing). 8⁰.
Corderius (M.). Colloquiorum Scholasticorum. 8⁰.
Hill (J.). Schrevelius, Lexicon. 8⁰.
Lily (W.). Short Introduction of Grammar. 8⁰.
Robertson (W.). Phraseologia Generalis. 8⁰.
[Rogers (T.).] Faith professed in the xxxix Articles. 4⁰.
Varenius (B.). Geographia Generalis (ed. Isaac Newton). Ed. 2. 8⁰.

1682

Almanacks (Culpepper, Dove, Pond, Swallow, Swan, Wing).
Barne (M.). Two University Sermons. 4⁰.
Bible. 4⁰.
N[ewman] (S.). Concordance. Ed. 3. F⁰.
Pindarick Poem to Duke of Albemarle. F⁰.
Puffendorf (S.). De officio hominis et civis. 8⁰.
Schuler (J.). Exercitationes ad principiorum Descartes primam partem. 8⁰.

1683

Barne (M.). University Sermon. 4⁰.
Beza (T.). Novum Testamentum. 24⁰.
Bible. 4⁰.
Burrell (J.). Sermon at Thetford. 4⁰.
Common Prayer. 4⁰.
Davenant (J.). De morte Christi. 12⁰.
Eusebius, etc. F⁰.
Hymenaeus Cantabrigiensis. (2 states.) 4⁰.
Jewel (J.). Apologia Ecclesiae Anglicanae. 12⁰.
North (J.). Plato, Dialogi selecti. Ed. 2. 8⁰.
Psalms in metre. 4⁰.
Robertson (W.). Manipulus Linguae Sanctae et Eruditorum. 8⁰.

1684

Barne (M.). Assize Sermon, Hertford. 4⁰.
Baronius (R.). Metaphysica. 12⁰.
Beda. Historia Ecclesiastica. F⁰.
Bullokar (J.). An English Expositour. Ed. 7. 8⁰.
Cambridge University Statutes. 8⁰.
Casimir (M.). Sarbievii Lyricorum libri IV. 24⁰.
Euripides. F⁰.
Naudaeus (G.). Bibliographica politica. 8⁰.
Stephanus (H.). Anacreon. 12⁰.
Whear (D.). De ratione et methodo legendi utrasque historias. 8⁰.
Winterton (R.). Poetae minores Graeci. 8⁰.

1685

Academiae Cantabrigiensis Affectus, decedente Carolo II. 4⁰.
Almanacks (Culpepper, Dove, Fly, Swallow). 8⁰.
Baron (R.). Metaphysica Generalis. 8⁰.
Castalio (S.). à Kempis, De Christo imitando. 12⁰.
Concordance.
Erasmus (D.). Enchiridion Militis Christiani. 12⁰.
Faber (T.). Longinus.
Gostwyke (W.). Sermon for victory over rebels. 4⁰.
Gower (H.). Discourse after death of Peter Gunning. 4⁰.
Hill (J.). Schrevelius, Lexicon. Ed. 6. 8⁰.
Lactantius. Opera. 8⁰.
Prayers for use in Trinity College Chapel. 4⁰.
Ray (J.). Second Appendix ad Catalogum.
Rhodokanakis (C.). De resolutione verborum. 8⁰.
Robertson (W.). Liber Psalmorum (Hebrew). (2 states.) 12⁰
Spencer (J.). De legibus Hebraeorum. F⁰.

1686

Almanack (Wing). 8⁰.
Articles of Enquiry. 4⁰.
Homer. Iliad. 8⁰.
Lucretius. 12⁰.
[(?) Newton (Isaac).] Tables for renewing College leases. 8⁰.
Novum Testamentum.
Robertson (W.). Manipulus Linguae Sanctae. 8⁰.
Schuler (J.). Exercitationes ad principiorum Descartes primam partem. 8⁰.
Sleidan (J.). De Quatuor Monarchiis. 12⁰.
Tertullianus, Apologeticus; Minucius Felix. 12⁰.
Thurlin (T.). Necessity of Obedience to Spiritual Governours. 4⁰.
Turner (F.). Letter to Clergy of Ely. 4⁰.
Wolf (H.). Isocrates, Orationes et Epistolae. 12⁰.

1687

Almanacks (Culpepper, Fly, Pond). 8⁰.
Ovid. Metamorphoses. 8⁰.
Vincentius Lirinensis. Commonitorium. 12⁰.

1688

Almanacks (Culpepper, Dove, Pond, Wing). 8⁰.
Barnes (J.). History of Edward III. F⁰.
Browne (T.). Concio ad Clerum. June. 4⁰.
„   Concio ad Clerum. July. 4⁰.
B[ullokar] (J.). An English Expositour. 12⁰.
Castalio (S.). à Kempis, De Christo imitando. 12⁰.
Illustrissimi Principis Ducis Cornubiae Genethliacon. 4⁰.
Musae Cantabrigienses. Wilhelmo et Mariae. 4⁰.
Sanderson (R.). Casus Conscientiae Novem. 8⁰.
[Saywell (W.).] The Reformation justified. Edd. 1 and 2. 4⁰.
„   The Office of a Chaplain. 4⁰.
Valla (L.). De linguae Latinae elegantia. 8⁰.
Widdrington (R.). Δεῖπνον καὶ Ἐπίδειπνον. 12⁰.

1689

Almanacks (Dove, Pond, Wing). 8⁰.
Fleetwood (W.). Sermon in King's College Chapel. 4⁰.
Homer. Iliad. 4⁰.
Launoius (J.). Epistolae. F⁰.
Musae Cantabrigienses. 4⁰.

1690

Fuller (S.). Canonica successio. 4⁰.
Hypomnemata didactica. 8⁰.
Milner (J.). De Nethinim sive Nethinaeis. 4⁰.

1691

Hanbury (N.). Supplementum analyticum ad aequationes Cartesianas. 4⁰.
Heyrick (T.). Miscellany Poems. 4⁰.
„   Submarine Voyage. 4⁰.
Power (T.). Paradise Lost 1 (Latin). 4⁰.
Walker (T.). Divine Hymns. 4⁰.

1692

Almanacks (Swallow, Wing). 8⁰.
Anatomy of a Jacobite. 4⁰.
De Merouville (P. C.). Cicero. Orationes Selectae (Delphini). 4⁰.
Edwards (J.). Enquiry into four remarkable texts of the N.T. 4⁰.
Eusebius, etc. F⁰.
Minellius (J.). Terentius, Comoediae. 12⁰.
Saywell (W.). The necessity of adhering to the Church of England. 4⁰.

1693

A new dictionary in five alphabets. 4⁰.
Jeffery (J.). Sermon at Norwich. 4⁰.
Knatchbull (Sir N.). Annotations upon difficult texts of N.T. 8⁰.
Robertson (W.). Phraseologia Generalis. 8⁰.
Russell (J.). Sermon. 4⁰.
Walker (T.). Assize Sermon. 4⁰.

1694

Almanacks (Pond, Swallow). 8º.
Barnes (J.). Euripides. Fº.
Elis (J.). Articulorum XXXIX Defensio. 12º.
Milner (J.). Defence of Archbishop Usher. 8º.

1695

Almanacks (Dove, Swallow). 8º.
Censorinus. De die natali. 8º.
Concordance. 12º.
Lacrymae Cantabrigienses in obitum Mariae. 4º.
Lily (W.). Short Introduction of Grammar. 8º.
Statuta legenda. Broadsheet. (n.d.)
Whitefoot (J.). A discourse on the power of charity. 8º.

1696

Almanacks (Culpepper, Dove, Pond, Wing). 8º.
Aristotle. De Poetica. 8º.
Busteed (M.). Orationes duae funebres. 12º.

1697

Aesop Naturaliz'd. 8º.
Ayloffe (W.). Oratio de Pace. 4º.
Gratulatio de redditu Gul. III. Fº.
Prognostication (Fly). 8º.

1698

Almanack (Fly). 8º.
Hutchinson (F.). Commencement Sermon. 4º.
N[ewman] (S.). Concordance. Ed. 4. Fº.
Nourse (P.). Commencement Sermon. 4º.
Ovid. Metamorphoses. 8º.
Psalms in metre. (Tate and Brady.) 8º.

1699

Almanacks (Culpepper, Dove, Fly, Pond, Swallow, Wing). 8º.
Cicero. Orationes (Delphini). 8º.
Edwards (J.). Commencement Sermon. 4º.
Leeds (E.). Methodus Graecam Linguam docendi. 8º.
Leng (J.). Sermon before the King at Newmarket. 4º.
Marsh (R.). Sermon at St Mary's. 4º.
Talbot (J.). Horatius. 4º.
Warren (Robt.). The Tablet of Cebes. 12º.

1700

Almanacks (Dove, Pond). 4º.
Bennet (T.). An Answer to the Dissenters' Pleas. Ed. 2. 8º.
Blackall (O.). Commencement Sermon. 4º.
Dillingham (W.). Vita Laurentii Chadertoni. 8º.
Edwards (J.). Contio et Determinatio pro gradu Doctoratus. 12º.
Gaskarth (J.). Commencement Sermon. 4º.
    „   Concio ad Clerum. 4º.

Hare (F.). Sermon at St Mary's. 4⁰.
Le Clerc (J.). Physica. 12⁰.
New Testament (Greek). 12⁰.
Philips (A.). Life of John Williams. 8⁰.
Syntaxis et Prosodia. 8⁰.
Tables for leases. Ed. 2. 8⁰.
Threnodia in obitum Ducis Glocestrensis. 12⁰.
Winterton (R.). Poetae minores Graeci. 8⁰.

1701

Alleyne (J.). Sermon at Loughborough. 4⁰.
Almanacks (Culpepper, Dove, Fly, Pond, Swallow, Wing). 8⁰.
Bennet (T.). Confutation of Popery. Edd. 1 and 2. 8⁰.
„   Answer to the Dissenters' Pleas. Ed. 3. 8⁰.
Cornwall (J.). Sermon at St Mary's. 4⁰.
Kettlewell (J.). Help to worthy communicating. Ed. 4. 8⁰.
Kuster (L.). De Suida Diatribe. 4⁰.
Laughton (J.). Vergilius, Bucolica, Georgica et Aeneis. 4⁰.
Leeds (E.). Veteres poetae citati ad P. Labbei sententiam. 12⁰.
Leng (J.). Terentius. Comoediae. Ed. 1. 4⁰. Ed. 2. 12⁰.
Marsden (R.). Concio ad Clerum. 4⁰.
Milner (J.). Animadversions upon Le Clerc's reflexions.
Neophytus. Oratio sancta ad Academiam. 4⁰.
Puffendorf (S.). De officiis Hominis et Civis. Ed. 6. 8⁰.
Talbot (J.). Horatius. Ed. 2. 12⁰.

1702

Almanacks (Culpepper, Dove, Fly, Pond, Swallow, Wing). 8⁰.
Annesley (W. A.). Catullus, Tibullus, Propertius. 4⁰.
Beaumont (J.). Psyche. Ed. 2. F⁰.
Bennet (T.). A Discourse of Schism. Edd. 1 and 2. 8⁰.
Buck (T.). The Augmentation of Poor Vicarages. 4⁰.
Curcellaeus (S.). Synopsis Ethices. 8⁰.
Descartes (R.). Ethice, in methodum et compendium. 8⁰.
Gassendus (P.). Institutio Astronomica. Ed. 6. 8⁰.
Laughton (J.). Vergilius, Bucolica, Georgica et Aeneis. Ed. 2. 12⁰.
Psalms in metre. (Brady and Tate.) 8⁰.
Stillingfleet (E.). Origines Sacrae. Ed. 7. F⁰.
Verses on the death of the King. F⁰.
Whiston (W.). Chronology of the Old Testament. 4⁰.
„   Harmony of the Four Evangelists. 4⁰.

1703

Bennet (T.). Defence of the Discourse of Schism. 8⁰.
„   Answer to Mr Shepherd's considerations. 8⁰.
Cellarius (C.). Notitia orbis antiqui. 4⁰.
Crispinus (D.). Ovidius de Tristibus. 8⁰.
Davies (J.). Maximus Tyrius. 8⁰.
Grotius de jure Belli et Pacis, Epitome. Ed. 2. 8⁰.
Piers (W.). Euripides, Medea et Phoenissae. 8⁰.
Whiston (W.). Tacquet, Elementa Geometriae. 8⁰.

1704

Bennet (T.). A Discourse of Schism. Ed. 3. 8⁰.
      ,,   Answer to Mr Shepherd's considerations. Ed. 2. 8⁰.
      ,,   Defence of the Discourse of Schism. Ed. 2. 8⁰.
Cassianus Bassus. 8⁰.
Le Clerc (J.). Logica. Ed. 4. 12⁰.
Leeds (E.). Lucian. 8⁰.
Leng (J.). Sermon at consecration of St Catharine's Chapel. 4⁰.
Needham (P.). Geoponica. 8⁰.
Ovid. Metamorphoses. 8⁰.
Savage (J.). Sermon at Welwyn. 4⁰.
      ,,   Assize Sermon at Hertford. 4⁰.
Sherwill (T.). Sermon on SS. Simon and Jude. Edd. 1 and 2. 4⁰.
      ,,   University Sermon. 4⁰.
Willymot (W.). Peculiar use of certain Latin words. 8⁰.

1705

Barnes (J.). Anacreon. 12⁰.
      ,,   Anacreon Christianus. 8⁰.
Bennet (T.). Confutation of Quakerism. 8⁰.
Cambridge Poll Book. F⁰.
Cicero. Epistolae Selectae. 8⁰.
Dawes (Sir W.). University Sermon. 4ᶜ.
Jeffery (J.). Sermon.
Kuster (L.). Suidas. Lexicon. F⁰.
Le Clerc (J.). Physica. Ed. 2. 8⁰.
Ovid. Epistolae. 8⁰.
St John (P.). Quatuor Orationes. 4⁰.
Stephens. Sermon.
Tixier (J.). Epistolae. 8⁰.
Whiston (W.). Sermon at Trinity Church. 4⁰.
Willymot (W.). Peculiar Use of certain Latin words. Ed. 2. 8⁰.
Woolston (T.). Old Apology revived. 8⁰.

1706

Bennet (T.). Confutation of Popery. Ed. 3. 8⁰.
Bouchery (W.). Hymnus Sacer e libro Judicum V. 4⁰.
Cicero. Orationes (Delphini). 8⁰.
Davies (J.). Caesar (Gr. and Lat.). 4⁰.
Dawson (J.). Lexicon to Greek Testament. 8⁰.
Ockley (S.). Introductio ad Linguas Orientales. 8⁰.
Snape (A.). Sermon before the Princess Sophia. 4⁰.
[Tudway (T.).] Anthems used in King's College Chapel. 8⁰.
Whiston (W.). Essay on Revelation of St John. 4⁰.

1707

Alleyne (J.). Sermon at Leicester. Edd. 1 and 2. 4⁰.
Almanacks (Dove, Pond, Wing). 8⁰.
[Bennet (T.).] Answer to the Dissenters' Pleas. Ed. 4. 8⁰.
      ,,   Necessity of Baptism. 8⁰.

Bentley (R.). Visitation Articles. 4⁰.
Cannon (R.). Sermon before the Queen at Newmarket. 4⁰.
Davies (J.). Minucius Felix. 8⁰.
[Jenkins.] Defensio S. Augustini. 8⁰.
Laughton (R.). Sheet of questions on Newtonian philosophy.
Newton (Sir I.). Arithmetica Universalis [ed. W. W.]. 8⁰.
Snape (A.). Commemoration Sermon in King's College Chapel. 4⁰.
Webb. Table of University Officers.
Whiston (W.). Praelectiones Astronomicae. 8⁰.

1708

Bennet (T.). Joint Use of precompos'd Forms of Prayer. Edd. 1 and 2. 8⁰.
    „   Discourse of Joint Prayer. Ed. 2. 8⁰.
Christian Manual of Devotions.
Epicedium in Georgium Annae conjugem. F⁰.
Johnson (T.). Sophocles, Antigone et Trachiniae. 8⁰.
Le Clerc (J.). Physica. Ed. 7. 12⁰.
Waller. Sermon at Bishop Stortford.
Whiston (W.). Accomplishment of Scripture Prophecies. 8⁰.
    „   New Theory of the Earth. Ed. 2. 8⁰.

1709

Bennet (T.). A Confutation of Quakerism. Ed. 2. 8⁰.
Bentley (R.). Emendationes ad Ciceronis Tusculanas. 8⁰.
Davies (J.). Cicero, Tusculanae Disputationes. 8⁰.
Needham (P.). Hierocles. 8⁰.
Sherwill (T.). Monarchy the best establishment. 4⁰.
Walker. Divine Essays.

1710

Hughes (J.). Chrysostom de Sacerdotio. 8⁰.
Laughton (R.). Philosophical Questions.
N. (J.). Compendium of Trigonometry. 12⁰.
Swift (J.). The Tale of a Nettle. Broadsheet.
Wasse (J.). Sallustius. 4⁰.
Webb (F.). Names of the Chancellors, etc. Broadsheet.
Whiston (W.). Praelectiones Physico-Mathematicae. 8⁰.
    „   Tacquet, Elementa Geometriae. Ed. 2. 8⁰.

1711

Barnes (J.). Homer. 4⁰.
Bentley (R.). Horatius. 4⁰.
Brome (E.). Christian Fasting. 8⁰.
Green (R.). Demonstration of the truth of the Christian Religion. 8⁰.
Herodotus, Vita Homeri. 4⁰.
Laughton (R.). Mathematical Lectures.

1712

Davies (J.). Minucius Felix et Commodianus. 8⁰.
Duport (J.) and Needham (P.). Theophrastus, Characteres. 8⁰.
Green (R.). Principles of Natural Philosophy. 8⁰.
Hughes (J.). Chrysostom de Sacerdotio. Ed. 2. 8⁰.
Ockley (S.). Oratio Inauguralis. 4⁰.

Peck. Essay on Study.
Quaestio Medica.
Thirlby (S.). Answer to Whiston's 17 Suspicions. 8⁰.
Varenius (B.). Geographia generalis. 8⁰.

1713

[Bentley (R.).] Emendationes in Menandri et Philemonis Reliquias. Ed. 2. 8⁰.
     „   Epistola de Johanne Malela. Ed. 2. 8⁰.
Bentley (T.). Notes on Bentley's Horace. 8⁰.
Drake (S.). Castilionis de Curiali sive Aulico. 8⁰.
Jesus College Statutes.
Massey (E.). Plato, de Republica. 8⁰.
Newton (Sir I.). Principia Mathematica. Ed. 2. 4⁰.
Oldham (G.). Sermon at Bishop Stortford. 4⁰.
Pycroft (S.). Enquiry into Freethinking. 8⁰.
Thirlby (S.). Defense of the Answer to Whiston. 8⁰.
Verses upon the Peace. F⁰.
Waterland (D.). Assize Sermon. Edd. 1 and 2. 4⁰.
Whiston (W.). Reflexions. Ed. 2. 8⁰.

1714

Acad. Cant. Carmina Funebria et Triumphalia. F⁰.
Bachelors' Statutes. 8⁰.
Potter (E.). Vindication of our Saviour's Divinity. 8⁰.
Pycroft (S.). Reflections on the Nature of Contentment. 8⁰.
Quaestiones una cum carminibus. 8⁰.
Statutes of the University. 8⁰.
Waller (J.). University Sermon. 4⁰.

1715

Acts of Parliament.
Aspinwall (E.). Preservative against Popery. 8⁰.
Bentley (R.). Sermon on Popery. 8⁰.
Clemens Alexandrinus.
Green. Sermon at Canterbury.
Innocency of Error. Ed. 2.
Puffendorf (S.). De Officio Hominis et Civis. 8⁰.
[S. (J.).] Herodotus, Clio. 8⁰.
Sermon (May 29).
Sherlock (T.). Sermon (Nov. 20, 1715). 4⁰.
Wright. Sermon (Nov. 5, 1715).

1716

Browne (Sir T.). Christian Morals. 12⁰.
Fleetwood (W.). Charge to the Clergy. Edd. 1 and 2. 4⁰.
Lyng (W.). Sermon at Yarmouth. 4⁰.
Needham (P.). University Sermon. 8⁰.
Pearce (Z.). Cicero de Oratore. 8⁰.
Proclamation. May 3.
Sturmy (D.). Discourses. 8⁰.
[Wake (W.).] Archbishop of Canterbury's Letter. 4⁰.
Waterland (D.). Thanksgiving Sermon. 8⁰.
Waterland (T.). Sermon on anniversary of King's accession. 8⁰.

1717

Laughton (R.). Sermon before the King at King's College Chapel. 2 eds. 8º.

1718

Bentley (T.). Cicero de Finibus, Paradoxa. 8º.
Colbatch (J.). Commemoration Sermon in Trinity College Chapel. 8º.
Crossinge (R.). Sermon (Peace and Joy). 8º.
Davies (J.). Cicero de Natura Deorum. 8º.
    „   Cicero de Finibus. 8º.
    „   Lactantius. Epitome. 8º.
Whitfield (J.). Assize Sermon at Ely. 8º.
Wotton (H.). Clemens Romanus. 8º.

1719

Booth. *Friendly Advice to Anabaptists.*
Elegiae Tristes ad pudicitiam exhortantes. 8º.
Needham (P.). Hierocles. 8º.
Plaifere (J.) and others. Tracts concerning Predestination. 8º.
Prior (M.). Verses. Fº sheet.
Waterland (D.). A vindication of Christ's divinity. Edd. 1 and 2. 8º.

1720

Cambridge Concordance. Fº.
Descartes (R.). Ethice. 8º.
Reading (W.). Socrates, Eusebius, Theodoritus. 3 vols. Fº.
Waterland (D.). An answer to Dr Whitby's reply. 8º.
    „   Eight sermons. Edd. 1 and 2. 8º.
    „   Vindication of Christ's divinity. Ed. 3. 8º.

1721

Barnes (J.). Anacreon. Ed. 2. 12º.
Davies (J.). Cicero, De Divinatione. 8º.
Declaration of the Vice-Chancellor and Heads, Feb. 27. Broadsheet.
[Gastrell (F.).] The Bishop of Chester's Case. Fº.
Maichelius (D.). Introductio ad Historiam Literariam. 8º.
Request about Tuition Fees, Feb. 27. Broadsheet.
Waterland (D.). Arian Subscription. Edd. 1 and 2. 8º.
    „   Vindication of Christ's divinity. Ed. 4. 8º.
    „   Sermon at St Paul's. 8º.

1722

Cotes (R.). Harmonia Mensurarum. 4º.
Covel (J.). Account of Greek Church. Fº.
Davies (J.). Cicero, De officiis. 8º.
Jortin (J.). Lusus Poetici. 4º.
King (J.). Epistola ad J. Friend. 8º.
Parne (T.). Sermon in Trinity. 8º.
Smith (J.). Beda, Historia Ecclesiastica. Fº.
Waterland (D.). Supplement to Arian Subscription. 8º.
Whiston (W.). Tacquet, Elementa Geometriae. Ed. 3. 8º.
Whitfield (J.). Visitation Sermon at Ely. 8º.

1723

Davies (J.). Cicero, Tusculanae Disputationes. Ed. 2. 8⁰.
    „   De Natura Deorum. Ed. 2. 8⁰.
Harę (F.). Cicero (Manutii).
Leng (J.). Terentius. Ed. 3. 12⁰.
Markland (J.). Epistola critica ad F. Hare. 8⁰.
Middleton (C.). Bibliothecae Cantabrigiensis Ordinandae Methodus. 4⁰.
Piers (W.). Euripides, Medea et Phoenissae. Ed. 2. 8⁰.
Short Introduction to Grammar, for the use of Bury School.
Shuckford (S.). Sermon at Norwich. 4⁰.

1724

Bentley (R.). Boyle Lecture Sermons. Ed. 5. 8⁰.
Doughty (G.). Sermon in King's College Chapel. Edd. 1 and 2. 4⁰.
Drake (S.). Concio ad Clerum. 4⁰.
[Gooch (T.).] Caius College Statutes. 8⁰.
Harding (C.). Vida Poetica.
Mason (C.). Oratio. 4⁰.
Newcome (J.). University Sermon. Edd. 1 and 2. 4⁰.
Parne (T.). Sermon at Bedford. 4⁰.
Rolfe (T.). Syllabus of Anatomy.
Waterland (D.). Critical History of Athanasian Creed. 4⁰.
Whitfield (J.). Sermon at St Mary's. 8⁰.

1725

Bentley (R.). Remarks upon a late Discourse of Free-Thinking. Ed. 6. 8⁰
Davies (J.). Cicero, Academica. 8⁰.
Dawson (J.). Lexicon to Greek Testament. Ed. 2. 8⁰.
Harris (S.). Oratio Inauguralis. 4⁰.
Poll for Knights of the Shire of the County of Cambridge.
Whitfield (J.). University Sermon. 8⁰.

1726

Arnald (R.). Sermon at Bishop Stortford. 4⁰.
Bentley (R.). Terentius, Phaedrus, Publilius Syrus. 4⁰.
Davies (J.). Curae Secundae in Caesaris Commentarios. 8⁰.
Hennebert (C.). Les Comédies de Térence. 12⁰.
King (J.). Euripides, Hecuba, Orestes, Phoenissae. 8⁰.
Knight (S.). Life of Erasmus. 8⁰.
Paris (J.). Miscellanea Pratico-Theoretica. 8⁰.

1727

Academiae Luctus in Obitum Georgii I. F⁰.
Basset (E.). Argument concerning Christian Revelation. 8⁰.
Chappelow (L.). Spencer, De legibus Hebraorum. 2 vols. F⁰.
Davies (J.). Cicero, De Legibus. 8⁰.
    „   Caesar, Opera. 4⁰.
Green (R.). Expansive and Contractive Forces. F⁰.
Inglis (A.). Bentivoglio's Letters in Italian. 8⁰.
Middleton (C.). Defensio. 4⁰.
Statutes. 8⁰.
Stebbing (H.). Polemical Tracts. F⁰.

1728

Aristotle, Poetica (Ed. Goulstoniana 2).
Battie (W.). Aristotelis Rhetorica. 8⁰.
Blomfield (B.). University Sermon. 8⁰.
[Chapman (J.).] Objections against Book of Daniel considered.
Davies (J.). Cicero, De Finibus. 8⁰.
Edwards (S.). Poem on Copernican System. 4⁰.
Hough (T.). Sermon at St Paul's School. 4⁰.
Long (R.). Commencement Sermon. Edd. 1 and 2. 4⁰.
[Newcome (S.).] Enquiry into evidence of Christian Religion. 8⁰.
Orders for Undergraduates. April 20.
Waterland (D.). Critical History of Athanasian Creed. Ed. 2. 8⁰.

1729

Baker (W.). Sermon preached at Lichfield. 4⁰.
Battie (W.). Isocrates. 8⁰.
Cicero, Orationes (Delphini). 8⁰.
Disney (J.). View of Ancient Laws against Immorality. F⁰.
Knight (S.). Spittall Sermon at St Bridget's. 4⁰.
Stebbing (H.). Defence of Confirmation. 4⁰.
Warren (M.). Epistle on Abuse of Bark in Fevers. 4⁰.

1730

Davies (J.). Cicero de Divinatione. Ed. 2. 8⁰.
    „   „   Tusculanae. Ed. 3. 8⁰.
Kent (N.). Excerpta ex Luciani operibus. 8⁰.
[Pope (A.).] Quaestiones una cum carminibus. 8⁰.
[Waterland (D.).] Advice to a young student. Ed. 2. 8⁰.

1731

[Chapman (J.).] Remarks on a letter to Dr Waterland. 8⁰.
[Gretton (P.).] Concio ad Clerum. 8⁰.
Johnson (T.). On Moral Obligation. 8⁰.
    „   University Sermon. 8⁰.
Law (E.). King's Origin of Evil. 4⁰.
Mounteney (R.). Demosthenes, Selectae orationes. 8⁰.
Trevigar (L.). Conic Sections. 4⁰.
[Waterland (D.).] Scripture Vindicated. Pt. II. 8⁰.
Welchman (E.). Tertullianus de Trinitate Liber. 8⁰.

1732

[Chapman (J.).] Remarks on Christianity as old as Creation. 8⁰.
Common Prayer. 8⁰.
Cotes (R.). Harmonia Mensurarum. 4⁰.
Crossinge (S.). Sermon before King William at Newmarket. 2 eds. 4⁰.
Davies (J.). Cicero de Natura Deorum. Ed. 2. 8⁰.
Gretton (P.). Conciones duae. 8⁰.
[Johnson (T.).] Quaestiones Philosophicae. 12⁰.
Pearce (Z.). Cicero, De Oratore. Ed. 2. 8⁰.
University Statutes. 8⁰.

1733

Chapman (J.). Remarks [cont.] on Christianity as old as Creation. 8⁰.
Colbatch (J.). Marriage-treaty between Charles II and Catherine. 4⁰.
Collection of Poems. 8⁰.
Common Prayer. 8⁰.
Davies (J.). Cicero de Natura Deorum. Ed. 3. 8⁰.
Excerpta e Statutis. 8⁰.
Gratulatio Acad. Cantab. Principis Auriaci nuptias celebrantis. F⁰.
Markland (J.) and Hare (F.). Epistola Critica. 8⁰.

1734

Chapman (J.). Examination of Sykes on Phlegon. 8⁰.
Clarke (Joseph). Further Examination of Dr Clarke on Space. 8⁰.
Clarkson (C.). Visitation Sermon at Melton Mowbray. 4⁰.
Guarini (G. B.). Il Pastor Fido. 4⁰.
Johnson (T.). Letter to Mr Chandler. 8⁰.
Law (E.). Enquiry into the ideas of Space, Time, etc. 8⁰.
Mason (C.). Oratio Woodwardiana. 4⁰.
[Rowning (J.).] Natural Philosophy. Pt. I. 8⁰.

1735

Bentley (R.). Boyle Lecture Sermons. Ed. 6. 8⁰.
Chapman (J.). Re-examination of Phlegon. 8⁰.
Johnson (T.). Puffendorf de Officiis. 12⁰.
     „   Quaestiones Philosophicae. Ed. 2. 8⁰.
Kerrich (S.). Commencement Sermon. 8⁰.
Kynnesman. Latin Grammar. Ed. 2.
Lyons (I.). Hebrew Grammar. 8⁰.
Middleton (C.). Origin of Printing in England. 4⁰.
Pastoral poem on the death of Lord How at Barbados. F⁰.
[Rowning (J.).] Natural Philosophy, Pt. II. 8⁰.
Sermon. April 2nd, 1733. 8⁰.
Waterland (D.). Discourse of Fundamentals. 8⁰.

1736

Davies (J.). Cicero, Academica. Ed. 2. 8⁰.
Gratulatio Acad. Walliae Principis nuptias celebrantis. F⁰.
Pastoral on the Death of Lord Howe. F⁰.
Pigg (T.). Assize Sermon at Thetford. 4⁰.
Warren (R.). Answer to Plain Account of Sacrament [by B. Hoadly]. 8⁰.

1737

Arnald (R.). Sermon at Leicester. 4⁰.
Bentley (R.). Remarks upon a late Discourse of Free-Thinking. Ed. 7. 8⁰.
Catalogue of Mr Johnson's books.
Muscut (J.). Visitation Sermon at Bedford.
Warren (R.). Appendix to Answer. 8⁰.
Waterland (D.). Review of Doctrine of Eucharist. 8⁰.

1738

Catalogue for a sale of books by Thurlbourn.
Davies (J.). Cicero, Disputationes Tusculanae. Ed. 4. 8⁰.

Lyons (I.). Hebrew Grammar. Ed. 2. 8⁰.
[Newcome (S.).] Nature and end of the Sacrament. 8⁰.
Pietas Acad. in funere Principis Wilhelminae Carolinae. F⁰.
Smith (R.). Compleat System of Opticks. 2 vols. 4⁰.
Williams (P.). University Sermon. 4⁰.

1739

Chapman (J.). Eusebius or the true Christian's Defense. 8⁰.
[Colbatch (J.).] Treatise for altering the present method of letting leases. 8⁰.
Cradock (J.). University Sermon. 4⁰.
Dunthorne (R.). Astronomy of the Moon. 8⁰.
Law (E.). King, Origin of Evil. Ed. 3. 8⁰.
Taylor (J.). Demosthenes. Proposals.
Weston (W.). Two Sermons. 8⁰.

1740

Saunderson (N.). Elements of Algebra. 2 vols. 4⁰.
Taylor (J.). Lysias. 8⁰.
    „   Appendix to Suidas. F⁰.

1741

Chapman (J.). De aetate Ciceronis de legibus. 8⁰.
Colbatch (J.). The Case of Proxies. 8⁰.
Davies (J.). Cicero de Finibus. Var. Ed. 2. 8⁰.
    „   „   de Divinatione. Ed. 3. 8⁰.
    „   „   de Legibus. 8⁰.
Davies (R.). Memoirs of Dr Nicholas Saunderson. 4⁰.
Garnett (J.). Assize Sermon. 4⁰.
Johnson (T.). Quaestiones Philosophicae. Ed. 3. 8⁰.
Keill (J.). Introductio ad veram Physicam. Ed. 6. 8⁰.
Squire (S.). Defense of the Antient Greek Chronology. 8⁰.
[„   ] The Ancient History of the Hebrews. 8⁰.
Taylor (J.). Demosthenes. Specimen only. 4⁰.
The Inward Call to the Holy Ministry.
Tunstal (J.). Epistola ad C. Middleton. 8⁰.

1742

Abridgement of Acts of Parliament relating to Excise. 8⁰.
Catalogue of Duplicates in Royal Library. 8⁰.
Long (R.). Astronomy. Vol. I. 4⁰.
Taylor (J.). Commentarius ad Legem Xviralem. 4⁰.

1743

Bally (G.). Solomon de Mundi Vanitate. 4⁰.
[Bentley (R.).] Remarks on a late discourse of Free-thinking. Ed. 8. 8⁰.
Bible. 12⁰.
Common Prayer 8⁰, 12⁰ and 32⁰.
Law (E.). Assize Sermon, Carlisle. 8⁰.
Newcome (J.). Sermon before the House of Commons. 4⁰.
Richardson (W.). Godwin. De praesulibus Angliae. F⁰.
Rutherforth (T.). Ordo Institutionum Physicarum. 4⁰.

Smart (C.). Carmen Alex. Pope in S. Caeciliam. Fº.
Taylor (J.). Demosthenes in Midiam et Lycurgus contra Leocratem. 8º.
      „   Marmor Sandvicense. 4º.
Wesley (S.). Poems. Ed. 2. 8º.

1744

Butler (S.). Hudibras. 2 vols. 8º.
Davies (J.). Cicero de Natura deorum. Ed. 4. 8º.
Grey (Z.). Review of Neal's History of the Puritans. 8º.
Parne (T.). University Sermon. 8º.
Psalms in metre. 32º.
Rutherforth (T.). Nature and obligations of virtue. 4º.
Squire (S.). Plutarchus de Iside et Osiride. 8º.

1745

A Day's Work of the Fates. 8º.
Bennet (P.). University Sermon. 8º.
Common Prayer. Fº, 8º and 12º.
Davies (J.). Cicero de Legibus. Ed. 2. 8º.
Dawes (R.). Miscellanea Critica. 8º.
Elstobb (W.). Pernicious consequences of replacing Sluices. 8º.
Garnett (J.). Commemoration Sermon. 4º.
Law (E.). Considerations on the state of the world. 8º.
Masters (R.). Sermon at Wilbraham. 8º.
Tryal of Jeroms and Footman. 8º.
Warner (M.). Sermon on the present rebellion. 8º.
      „   Fast Sermon. 8º.
Williams (P.). Sermon at Starston. 8º.

1746

[A Divine.] Nature and Necessity of Catechising. 8º.
Bateman (W.). Concio ad Clerum. 4º.
Bible (Welsh). 8º.
Kerrich (S.). Thanksgiving Sermon. 8º.
Knowles (T.). The existence and attributes of God. 8º.
Mays (C.). Thanksgiving Sermon. 8º.
[Powell (W. S.).] Heads of Lectures in Experimental Philosophy. 8º.
Psalms (Welsh). 8º.
Rutherforth (T.). Determinatio Quaestionis Theologicae. 4º.
      „   Sermon before the House of Commons. 4º.
Smart (C.). Carmen Alex. Pope in S. Caeciliam Latine redditum. Ed. 2. 4º.
Warner (M.). Thanksgiving Sermon. 8º.
Warren (Rich.). Mutual duty of minister and people. 4º.
Weston (W.). Rejection of Christian Miracles by Heathens. 8º.
      „   Moral impossibility of conquering England. 8º.
      „   Three Sermons. Ed. 2. 8º.

1747

Bible. 12º.
Cotes (R.). Hydrostatical and Pneumatical Lectures. Ed. 2. 8º.
Heathcote (R.). Historia Astronomiae. 8º.

1748

Brooke (Z.). Defensio Miraculorum. 4°.
Common Prayer. F°, 12°. (2 eds.)
Excerpta e Statutis. 8°.
Goodall (H.). Duties attending a proper discharge of the Ministry. 4°.
Gratulatio Acad. Cant. de reditu Georgii II. F°.
Psalms in metre. 12°. (2 eds.)
Rutherforth (T.). System of Natural Philosophy. 2 vols. 4°.
Taylor (J.). Demosthenes. Vol. III. 4°.
Weston (W.). On the remarkable wonders of antiquity. 8°.

1749

Beaumont (J.). Poems. 4°.
Bennet (P.). Two University Sermons. 8°.
Fauchon (J.). A publick lecture to La Butte. 4°.
Green (J.). Commencement Sermon. 4°.
Law (E.). Considerations on the state of the world. Ed. 2. 8°.
   „   Discourse upon the life of Christ. 8°.
Mason [W.]. Installation Ode. 4°.
Moody (S.). Concio Academica. 8°.
Psalms in metre. 12°.
[Ross (J.).] Cicero, Epistolae. 8°.
Smith (R.). Harmonics. 8°.
Taylor (J.). Sermon at Bishop-Stortford. 4°.

1750

Chapman (T.). On the Roman Senate. 8°.
Common Prayer. 12°.
[Grey (Z.).] Historical account of Earthquakes. 8°.
Hubbard (H.). Sermon at Ipswich. 4°.
Knowles (T.). Existence and Attributes of God. 8°.
[Masters (R.).] List of...members of Corpus Christi College. 4°.
Michell (J.). Treatise of artificial magnets. 8°.
Orders and Regulations. Broadsheet.
Rutherforth (T.). Defence of [Sherlock's] discourses. Edd. 1 and 2. 8°.
Smart (C.). On the Eternity of the Supreme Being. 4°.

1751

Barford (W.). Dissertatio. 4°.
Common Prayer. 8° and 12°.
Luctus in Obitum Frederici. F°.
Michell (J.). Treatise of artificial magnets. Ed. 2. 8°.
Mickleborough (J.). Sermon. 8°.
Offices. 8°.
Psalms in metre. 12°.
Rutherforth (T.). Discourse on Credibility of Miracles. 4°.
Smart (C.). On the Immensity of the Supreme Being. 4°.
Synopsis compendiaria. 8°.
Van-Sampson (I.). David's Prophecy relating to C——b——ge. 8°.
? Elstobb (W.). References to Map of Sutton. 8°.

1752

Bible. 12º.
Chappelow (L.). Commentary on Job. 2 vols. 4º.
Common Prayer. Fº, 8º and 12º.
Foster (J.). Oratio. 4º.
Gilbert (Sir G.). Abstract of Locke. 8º.
Green (J.). Sermon. 4º.
Psalms in metre. 8º.
Smart (C.). On the Eternity of the Supreme Being. Ed. 2. 4º.
„   On the Omniscience of the Supreme Being. 4º.

1753

Common Prayer. 8º and 12º.
Green (W.). Song of Deborah. 4º.
Hingeston (R.). Progymnasmata hellenica. 8º.
Hurd (R.). Charity Schools Sermon. 8º.
Kedington (R.). Sermon. 4º.
Masters (R.). History of Corpus Christi College. 4º.
Offices. 8º.
Peckard (P.). Sermon at Huntingdon. 8º.
[Powell (W. S.).] Heads of Lectures in Experimental Philosophy. 8º.
Rutherforth (T.). Concio ad Clerum. 4º.
Smart (C.). On the Immensity of the Supreme Being. Ed. 2. 4º.

1754

Common Prayer. Fº, 4º and 12º.
Dockwray (T.). Sermon at Newcastle. 8º.
Elstobb (W.). Remarks on a Pamphlet. 8º.
Kedington (R.). Sermons. 8º.
Psalms in metre. 4º and 12º.
Reasons against a Bill for...deepening...the River Nene. 8º.
Rutherforth (T.). Institutes of Natural Law. Vol. 1. 8º.
Smart (C.). On the Power of the Supreme Being. 4º.

1755

Baker (G.). Dissertatio. 4º.
Bally (G.). On the Justice of the Supreme Being. 4º.
Carmina ad nobil. Thomam Holles. Fº.
Common Prayer. 8º and 12º.
Edwards (T.). Hare's Translation of the Psalms. 8º.
Green (W.). Trans. of Habakkuk. 4º.
Hallam (J.). Dissertatio. 4º.
Law (E.). Considerations on Religion. Ed. 3. 8º.
[Montagu (F.).] Oratio. 4º.
Paris (J.). Oratio. 4º.
Psalms in metre. 8º.
Skynner (J.). Oratio...coram Thoma Holles. Fº and 4º.
Taylor (J.). Elements of Civil Law. 4º.

1756

Bally (G.). On the Wisdom of the Supreme Being. 4º.
Barford (W.). Oratio. 4º.

Bell (W.). Dissertation. 4⁰.
Bentham (J.). Catalogue of the Principal Members of Ely. 4⁰.
Bible. 12⁰.
Collignon (C.). Compendium Anatomico-Medicum. 4⁰.
Common Prayer. 8⁰ and 12⁰.
[Grey (Z.).] Farther account of memorable Earthquakes. 8⁰.
Mason (W.). Odes. Edd. 1 and 2. 4⁰.
Pennington (J.). Sermon at Huntingdon. 8⁰.
Ross (J.). Commencement Discourse. 4⁰.
Rutherforth (T.). Institutes of Natural Law. Vol. II. 8⁰.
      ,,   Ordo Institutionum Physicarum. Ed. 2. 4⁰.
Smart (C.). On the Eternity of the Supreme Being. Ed. 3. 4⁰.
     ,,   On the Goodness of the Supreme Being. 4⁰.
     ,,   On the Omniscience of the Supreme Being. Ed. 2. 4⁰.

1757

[Bentham (J.).] Queries offered to Inhabitants of Ely. 8⁰.
Common Prayer. F⁰, 8⁰ and 12⁰.
Dickens (C.). Sermon at Hemingford. 4⁰.
Glynn (R.). The Day of Judgment. Edd. 1 and 2. 4⁰.
Hurd (R.). Horatii Epistolae. Ed. 3. 2 vols. 8⁰.
     ,,   Letter to Mr Mason. 8⁰.
Lyons (I.). Hebrew Grammar. Ed. 2. 8⁰.
Ockley (S.). History of the Saracens. 2 vols. Ed. 3. 8⁰.
Psalms in metre. 12⁰.
Taylor (J.). Demosthenes. Vol. II. 4⁰.

1758

Backhouse (J.). Sermon. 4⁰.
Bally (G.). On the Providence of the Supreme Being. 4⁰.
Bible. 12⁰.
Chappelow (L.). Translation of Abu Ismael's The Traveller. 4⁰.
Common Prayer. 4⁰ and 12⁰.
Glynn (R.). The Day of Judgment. Ed. 3. 4⁰.
Hadley (J.). Plan of a Course of Chemical Lectures. 8⁰.
Law (E.). King, Origin of Evil. Ed. 4. 2 vols. 8⁰.
Newton (B.). Sermon. 4⁰.
Ogden (S.). Two University Sermons. 4⁰.
Psalms in metre. 4⁰.
Roberts (W.). Dissertatio. 4⁰.

1759

Baskerville (J.). Specimen of Holy Bible with Proposals. F⁰.
Bible. 12⁰.
Common Prayer. 8⁰ and 12⁰.
Edwards (T.). Doctrine of Irresistible Grace. 8⁰.
Excerpta e Statutis. 8⁰.
Heathcote (R.). Concio ad Clerum. 4⁰.
Observations on present state of the...Universities. 8⁰.
Pilkington (M.). Remarks on Passages in Scripture. 8⁰.
Porteus (B.). Death, a poem. Edd. 1 and 2. 4⁰.

1760

Baskerville (J.). Specimen of Holy Bible with Proposals. F⁰.
Bible. 8⁰ and 12⁰.
Common Prayer. F⁰, 8⁰ and (Baskerville) 8⁰.
Gordon (J.). New Estimate of Manners. Pts. I and II. 8⁰.
Hallifax (S.). Three Discourses. 8⁰.
Lort (M.). University Sermon. 8⁰.
Luctus...et Gratulationes. F⁰.
Muscut (J.). Sermons. 8⁰.
Porteus (B.). Death, a poem. Ed. 3. 4⁰.
Psalms in metre. 8⁰.
Scott (J.). Heaven, a vision. 4⁰.
Waring (E.). Letter to Dr Powell. 8⁰.
    „   Reply to...[Dr Powell's]...Pamphlet. 8⁰.
[Waterland (D.).] Advice to a young Student. 8⁰.
[Wilson (J.).] Vindication of Miscellanea Analytica. 8⁰.

1761

Academicus. A Letter to Mr George Whitefield. 8⁰.
Bible. 12⁰.
Common Prayer (Baskerville). 8⁰.
[Gordon (J.).] New Estimate of Manners. Pt. III. 8⁰.
Gratulatio Acad. Cant. Nuptias celebrantis. F⁰.
[Green (J.).] Letter to G. Whitefield. Edd. 1 and 2. 8⁰.
Newcome (H.). Table of Cautions, Fees and Perquisites. F⁰.
Porteus (B.). Discourse. 8⁰.
Rutherforth (T.). Letter to Mr Kennicott. 8⁰.
Scott (J.). Heaven, a vision. Ed. 2. 4⁰.
    „   Odes on Several Subjects. 4⁰.
    „   Purity of Heart. Edd. 1 and 2. 4⁰.

1762

Address to Ferdinand IV, King of the Two Sicilies. Broadsheet.
Anstey (C.) and Roberts (W. H.). Gray's Elegy in Latin. 4⁰.
Bible. F⁰, 4⁰ and 12⁰.
Common Prayer. F⁰, 8⁰ and 12⁰ and (Baskerville) 8⁰ and 12⁰.
Edwards (T.). Dissertation. 8⁰.
Gratulatio Acad. Cant. natales Georgii. F⁰.
Green (W.). Trans. of the Psalms. 8⁰.
Hallifax (S.). Three Discourses. Ed. 2. 8⁰.
Pickering (D.). The Statutes at Large. Vols. 1–3. 8⁰.
Rutherforth (T.). Second Letter to Dr Kennicott. 8⁰.
Scott (J.). Hymn to Repentance. 4⁰.
Waring (E.). Miscellanea analytica. 4⁰.

1763

Backhouse (W.). University Sermon. Ed. 1. 8⁰. Ed. 2. 4⁰.
Bible (Baskerville). F⁰.
Brooke (Z.). Several Discourses. 8⁰.
    „   Two University Sermons. Edd. 1 and 2. 4⁰
Cantabrigia depicta. 2 eds. 12⁰.
Collignon (C.). Introduction to Anatomy. 8⁰.

Collignon (C.). Happiness, an Epistle to a Friend. 4º.
  „   Messiah, a sacred Poem. 4º.
Common Prayer and Psalms. 12º.
Delap (J.). Concio ad Clerum. 4º.
Gratulatio Acad. Cant. in Pacem. Fº.
Hey (J.). The Redemption. 4º.
Hubbard (H.). Charity Sermon. Ed. 2. 4º.
[Martyn (T.).] Account of the late donation of a Botanic Garden, with Rules and Orders. 4º.
Pickering (D.). Statutes. Vols. 4–8, 25–26. 8º.
Rutherforth (T.). Four Charges to Clergy. 8º.
S[andys] (G.). Juvenalis Satyrae. 8º. 2 eds.
Shepherd (A.). Heads of Lectures in Experimental Philosophy. (2 pts.) 8º.
[Vickers (W.).] Companion to Altar. 12º.

1764

Bible. 8º.
Collignon (C.). Structure of Human Body. Edd. 1 and 2. 8º.
Common Prayer and Psalms. 4º, 8º and 12º.
[? Hutchinson (T.).] Address to Clergy. 8º.
Long (R.). Astronomy. Vol. II. 4º.
Mainwaring (J.). University Sermon. 4º.
Pickering (D.). Statutes. Vols. 9–13. 8º.
Primatt (W.). Accentus Redivivi. 8º.

1765

Act for making Cam more navigable. 8º.
Bible. 4º, 8º and 12º.
Collignon (C.). Reflections on Art of Physic. 8º.
Cranwell (J.). Trans. of Browne's Immortality of the Soul. 4º.
Edwards (T.). Epistola ad R. Lowth. 8º.
[Jebb (J.).] Excerpta e Newtoni Principiis. 4º.
Law (E.). Considerations on Religion. Ed. 5. 8º.
Lettice (J.). Conversion of St Paul. 4º.
[Martyn (T.).] Proposal for an Annual Subscription for the Botanic Garden, with Account of the Donation. 4º.
Offices. 8º.
Pickering (D.). Statutes. Vols. 14–20. 8º.
Psalms. 12º.
Psalms in metre. 12º.
Rutherforth (T.). Concio ad Clerum. 4º.
Shepherd (A.). Heads of Lectures in Experimental Philosophy. Re-issue. 8º.
Zouch (T.). The Crucifixion. 4º.

1766

Analysis of Locke's Doctrine of Ideas. 4º.
Barnardiston (J.). Sermon before the Commons. 4º.
Common Prayer and Psalms. 8º and 12º.
Explanation of the Affirmative and Negative Signs in Algebra. 8º.
Harrison (J.). Method of making Fen Banks impregnable. 8º.
Jenner (C.). Poems. 4º.

Matty (H.). Oratio. 4⁰.
Pickering (D.). Statutes. Vols. 21–23. 8⁰.
Psalms. 4⁰.
Rules for Addenbrooke's Infirmary. 8⁰.
Rutherforth (T.). Vindication...concerning Subscription. 8⁰.
     ,,   2nd Vindication. 8⁰.
Walton (W.). Sermon at Huntingdon. 4⁰.

1767

Bible. 8⁰ and 12⁰.
Bryant (J.). Observations...on Ancient History. 4⁰.
Chappelow (L.). Trans. of Six Assemblies. 8⁰.
Churchill (F.). Oratio. 4⁰.
Common Prayer and Psalms. F⁰, 8⁰ and 12⁰.
Farmer (R.). Essay on Learning of Shakespeare. Edd. 1 and 2. (2 states.) 8⁰.
Firebrace (J.). Sermon at Stowmarket. 8⁰.
Gordon (J.). Sermon. 4⁰.
Jenner (C.). The Gift of Tongues. 4⁰.
Nevile (T.). Virgil's Georgics. 8⁰.
Pickering (D.). Statutes. Vol. 27. 8⁰.
Raikes (R.). Oratio. 4⁰.
Roe (J.). Twenty Sermons. Ed. 2. 8⁰.
Rutherforth (T.). Defence of a Charge. 8⁰.
Tutor's Petition. Broadsheet.

1768

Ashton (C.). S. Justini Apologiae. 8⁰.
Bible. 4⁰ and 8⁰.
Common Prayer and Psalms. 4⁰ and 12⁰.
Cranwell (J.). Trans. of Vida's The Christiad. 8⁰.
Edwards (T.). Two Dissertations. 8⁰.
Hallifax (S.). Two University Sermons. 4⁰.
Jenner (C.). The Destruction of Nineveh. 4⁰.
Lot Book of Fen Lands Commissioners. 8⁰.
Lyons (I.). Observations on Scripture History. 8⁰.
[Marriott (J.).] Argument...on Poor Rate. 8⁰.
Martyn (T.). Sermon. 4⁰.
Pickering (D.). Statutes. Vol. 28. 8⁰.
Watson (R.). Institutionum Chemicarum Pars I. 4⁰.

1769

Bible. 4⁰, 8⁰ and 12⁰.
Collignon (C.). Moral and Medical Dialogues. 8⁰.
     ,,   Medical and Moral Tracts. (Title-page only.) 8⁰.
Common Prayer and Psalms. 4⁰ and 8⁰.
Favell (J.). Review of Abraham's Case. 4⁰.
Goddard (P. S.). Sermon at Clare Hall. 8⁰.
[Gray (T.).] Installation Ode. 4⁰.
Hallifax (S.). Sermon before the Commons. 4⁰.
     ,,   Heads of Lectures in Roman Civil Law. 8⁰.
[Law (E.).] Defence of Locke's Personal Identity. 8⁰.
[Lort (M.).] Projecte conteyninge the State...of the Universitie. 4⁰.
Ludlam (W.). Astronomical Observations. 4⁰.

Marriott (J.). Rights...of the Universities defended. 8⁰.
„   Argument...on Poor Rate. 8⁰.
Nevile (T.). Imitations. Vol. II. 8⁰.
Pickering (D.). Statutes. Vol. 24. 8⁰.
Taylor (J.). Demosthenes. 2 vols. 4⁰.
Watson (R.). Assize Sermon. 4⁰.

1770

Bible. 12⁰.
Common Prayer. F⁰, 4⁰ and 12⁰.
Excerpta e Statutis Acad. Cant. 8⁰.
Form of Prayer for Addenbrooke's. 8⁰.
Hodson (W.). The Temple of Solomon. 4⁰.
Jebb (J.). Account of Theological Lectures. 4⁰.
[Law (E.).] Observations...about Literary Property. 8⁰.
Lort (M.). Sermon at Lambeth. 4⁰.
Ludlam (W.). Mathematical Essays. 8⁰.
[Martyn (T.).] Chronological Series of Engravers. 8⁰.
Ogden (S.). Sermons on Prayer. 2 eds. 8⁰.
Prescot (K.). St Paul at Athens. 8⁰.
Psalms in metre. 12⁰.
Tyson (M.). Account of a MS. at Corpus. 4⁰.
„   Poems. 4⁰.
Waring (E.). Meditationes algebraicae. 4⁰.
Wheeldon (J.). Monody. 4⁰.

1771

Bentham (J.). History...of Ely. 4⁰.
Collignon (C.). Structure of Human Body. Ed. 3. 8⁰.
Common Prayer. 12⁰.
Gordon (J.). Sermon. 4⁰.
Hallifax (S.). Addenbrooke's Sermon. 4⁰.
Martyn (T.). Catalogus Horti Botan. Cant. 8⁰.
Pickering (D.). Statutes. Vol. 29. 8⁰.
[Prescot (Ch.).] Catalogue of St Catharine's Library. 4⁰.
Rutherforth (T.) Addenbrooke's Sermon. 4⁰.
Stevens (T.). Two University Sermons. 8⁰.
Watson (R.). Essay on Chemistry. 8⁰.
„   Plan of Chemical Lectures. 8⁰.

1772

Gibson (W.). Conscience. Edd. 1 and 2. 4⁰.
Hallifax (S.). 3 University Sermons. Edd. 1 and 2. 4⁰. Ed 3. 8⁰.
[?] Letters to above on above. Edd. 1 and 2. 4⁰.
Jebb (J.). Account of Theological Lectures. Ed. 2. 4⁰.
Martyn (T.). Mantissa plantarum. 8⁰.
Peckard (P.). Sermon at Huntingdon. 4⁰.
Powell (W. S.). Commencement Sermon. Ed. 4. 8⁰.
Purkis (W.). Assize Sermon at Wisbech. 4⁰.
Shepherd (A.). Astronomical Tables. 4⁰.
Waring (E.). Algebraical Curves. 4⁰.
Wheeldon (J.). Two Sermons. 8⁰.

1773

Alphonso. a Poem. 4⁰.
Bible. 8⁰ and 12⁰.
Burrough (H.). Lectures on Church Catechism. Edd. 1 and 2. 8⁰.
Churchill (F.). Concio ad Clerum. 4⁰.
Edwards (T.). University Sermon. 8⁰.
Hey (J.). Assize Sermon. 8⁰.
[Hey (R.).] Thoughts on Duelling. 4⁰.
Jebb (J.). Remarks on Education. Edd. 1, 2 and 3. 8⁰.
„   University Sermon. 8⁰.
Layard (C. P.). Charity. 4⁰.
Mainwaring (J.). Sermon. 4⁰.
Pickering (D.). Statutes. Vol. 30. 8⁰.
Powell (W. S.). Charge to the Clergy. 8⁰.
Prescot (K.). Letters concerning Homer. 4⁰.
Tyson (M.). Account of a Horn at Corpus. 4⁰.
Wheeldon (J.). Sermon at Huntingdon Assizes. 4⁰.

1774

Bible. 12⁰.
Gould (W.). Concio ad Clerum. 4⁰.
Hallifax (S.). Lectures on Roman Law. 8⁰.
Hey (J.). Sermons. 8⁰.
[Jebb (J.).] Plan for Public Examinations. F⁰.
[Law (E.).] Considerations on subscribing. 8⁰.
Law (E.). Considerations on Religion. Ed. 6. 8⁰.
Nevile (T.). Imitations. Vol. 1. Ed. 2. 8⁰.
„   Virgil's Georgics. Ed. 2. 8⁰.
[Powell (W. S.).] Observations on Annual Examinations. 8⁰.
[Prescot (K.).] Shakespeare, [an Essay]. 4⁰.
Sleidan (J.). De Quatuor Monarchiis. 8⁰.
Taylor (J.). Demosthenes. Vols. ii and iii, titles only. 4⁰.

1775

Bible. 12⁰.
Craven (W.). University Sermon. 8⁰.
„   Sermons. 8⁰.
Hallifax (S.). Heads of lectures on Roman Law. Ed. 2. 8⁰.
Hayes (S.). Duelling. 4⁰.
[Heckford (R.).] Discourse. 8⁰.
Layard (C. P.). Duelling. 4⁰.
Mainwaring (J.). University Sermon. 4⁰.
Martyn (T.). Elements of Natural History. 8⁰.
Mills (J.). Plato's Apology. 8⁰.
Pickering (D.). Statutes. Vol. 31. 8⁰.

1776

Cantabrigia depicta. 12⁰.
Cockman (T.). Tully's Offices. Ed. 9. 8⁰.
Comber (T.). Treatise of Laws. 8⁰.
Cooper (S.). University Sermon. 4⁰.
Green (W.). Trans. of Isaiah lii. 4⁰.

Hayes (S.). Prophecy. 4º.
Hubbard (H.). Sermon at Ipswich. New ed. 4º.
Jebb (J.). Address on Public Examinations. 8º.
Law (E.). Reflections on Life of Christ, with Appendix by W. Paley. 8º.
Love Elegies. 4º.
Mainwaring (J.). Sermon at Church Stretton. 4º.
New Testament.
Spelman (E.). Xenophon. Ed. 3. 2 vols. 8º.
[Stevens (W.).]. Strictures on Watson's Sermon. 8º.
Wakefield (G.). Poemata. 4º.
Waring (E.). Meditationes analyticae. 4º.
Warren (J.). Addenbrooke's Sermon. 4º.
Watson (R.). Apology for Christianity. 8º.
     „   University Sermon (June). Ed. 1. 4º. Edd. 2 and 3. 8º.
             Remarks on above by an Undergraduate. 4º.
             Vindication of Dr W——n. 4º.
     „   University Sermon (October). 4º.
Weston (E.). Family Discourses (ed. C. Weston). Ed. 2. 8º.

1777

Bible. 12º.
Cole (W.). Sermon at Eynesbury. 4º.
Common Prayer. 12º.
Cooper (S.). Sermon. 4º.
Hayes (S.). Prayer. 4º.
Hey (J.). Addenbrooke's Sermon. 4º.
Nasmith (J.). Catalogue of MSS. at Corpus. 4º.
Ogden (S.). Sermons on Ten Commandments. 8º.
     „   Sermons on Christian Faith. 8º.
Paley (W.). Sermon. 4º.
Psalms. 4º.
[Stevens (W.).] Strictures on Watson's Sermon. Ed. 2. 8º.
     „   Answer to Dr Watson. 8º.
Wandesforde (Sir C.). Instructions to his son. Vol. 1. 12º.
Watson (R.). Apology for Christianity. Ed. 2. 4º and 12º.

1778

Bible. 8º and 12º.
Comber (T.). Memoirs of Lord Wandesforde. (Instructions, Vol. 11.)
    Edd. 1 and 2. 12º.
Common Prayer. 4º.
[? Harrison (J.).] Considerations on Fens near Ely. 8º.
Hayes (S.). The Nativity. 4º.
Hey (J.). Sermon. 8º.
Isola (A.). Trans. of Italian Poets. 8º.
Mainwaring (J.). Sermon. 4º.
Nasmith (J.). Itineraria Symonis Simeonis. 8º.
Part of Dr Woodward's Will. 8º.
Pickering (D.). Statutes. Vol. 32. 8º.
Rennell (T.). Oratio. 4º.
Rules of Addenbrooke's Hospital. 4º.
Smith (R.). Elementary Optics. 4º.

1779

Beausobre (I. de). New Version of St Matthew. 8⁰.
Bible. 8⁰.
Common Prayer. 12⁰.
Edwards (J.). Theocritus Idyllia. 8⁰.
Evasion of Payments, a discourse. 8⁰.
A Layman. Reflections on....Death. 8⁰.
Malden (H.). King's College Chapel. Ed. 3. 8⁰.
[Matthias (T. J.).] Oratio. 4⁰.
Psalms. 12⁰.
Rutherforth (T.). Institutes of Natural Law. Ed. 2. 8⁰.
Waring (E.). Meditationes algebraicae. Ed. 2. 4⁰.

1780

Common Prayer. F⁰, 8⁰ and 12⁰.
Cooke (W.). Concio ad Clerum. 4⁰.
„   University Sermon (February). 4⁰.
„   University Sermon (April). 4⁰.
„   University Sermon (June). 4⁰.
Hayter (T.). Remarks on Hume's Dialogues. 8⁰.
Hughes (T.). The Ascension. 4⁰.
Mainwaring (J.). Sermons and Dissertation. 8⁰.
Milner (I.). Plan of Lectures on Chemistry. 8⁰.
Morgan (C.). Sermon at Ely. 4⁰.
Ogden (S.). Sermons. 2 vols. Ed. 2. 8⁰.
Pickering (D.). Statutes. Vol. 33. 8⁰.
Watson (R.). Discourse at Ely. 4⁰.
„   University Sermon. Edd. 1, 2 and 3. 4⁰. Ed. 4. 8⁰.

1781

Cantabrigia depicta. 12⁰.
Cooke (W.). University Sermon. 4⁰.
Gibson (W.). Jerusalem destroyed. 4⁰.
„   Religion. 4⁰.
Green (W.). Poetical parts of O.T. translated. 4⁰.
Locke (J.). Conduct of the Understanding. 8⁰. (2 issues.)
[Mainwaring (J.).] Essay on Methodism. 8⁰.
Morgan (C.). Sermon at Ely. 4⁰.
Postlethwaite (T.). Discourse. 4⁰.
Vince (S.). Conic Sections. 8⁰.
Watson (R.). Chemical Essays. Vols. I and II. 8⁰.

1782

[Brundish (J. J.).] Elegy on a Family Tomb. 4⁰.
Excerpta e Statutis. 8⁰.
Madan (S.). Call of the Gentiles. 4⁰.
Martyn (T.). Heads of Lectures in Natural History. 8⁰.
Pickering (D.). Statutes. Vol. 34. 8⁰.
Plumptre (R.). Hints respecting University Officers. 8⁰.
Psalms (Tate and Brady). 12⁰. (2 issues.)

Thoughts on a Pre-existent State. 8º.
Waring (E.). Meditationes algebraicae. Ed. 3. 4º.
Watson (R.). Chemical Essays. Vol. III. 8º.

1783

Bible. 12º. (N.T., 1784.)
Craven (W.). Sermons. 8º.
Dickens (C.). Sermon at St Ives. 4º.
Hayes (S.). Hope. 4º.
Hey (J.). Heads of Lectures in Divinity. 8º.
Hey (R.). Dissertation on Gaming. 8º.
[Isola (A.).] J. J. B[rundish]'s Elegy in Italian. 4º.
Morgan (C.). Poems. 4º.
Peckard (P.). University Sermon. 4º.
Poem on the Love of our neighbour. 4º.

1784

Atwood (G.). Treatise on Rectilinear Motion. 8º.
Barford (W.). Concio ad Clerum. 4º.
Dickens (C.). Sermon at Hemingford Grey. 4º.
Hayes (S.). The Creation. 4º.
Hey (R.). Dissertation on Gaming. Ed. 2. 8º.
      „   Dissertation on Duelling. 8º.
Isola (A.). Translations of Italian Poets. Ed. 2. 8º.
Lloyd (T.). Norrisian Prize Essay. 4º.
Masters (R.). Memoirs of Thomas Baker and Catalogue of his MSS. 8º.
Milner (I.). Plan of Chemical Lectures. 8º.
Parkinson (T.). Sermon. 4º.
Peckard (P.). University Sermon. 4º.
Remarks on address to Governors of Addenbrooke's. 4º.
Seale (J. B.). Analysis of Greek Metres. 8º.

1785

Common Prayer. 12º.
Concise Description of the Town and University. 12º.
Cooke (W.). Aristotle, de Poetica. 8º.
Excerpta e Statutis. 8º.
Hayes (S.). The Exodus. 4º.
Hey (R.). Dissertation on Suicide. 8º.
Howe (J.) and Grosvenor (B.). Discourses. 8º.
Hutchinson (T.). Xenophon. Ed. 4. 4º.
Ludlam (W.). Rudiments of Mathematics. 8º.
Parkinson (T.). System of Mechanics. 4º.
A Questionist. Ten Minutes Advice to Freshmen. 12º.
Relhan (R.). Flora cantabrigiensis. 8º.
Statuta Academiae Cantabrigiensis. 4º.
Waring (E.). Meditationes analyticae. Ed. 2. 4º.
Watson (R.). Theological Tracts. Vols. I–III, VI. 8º.
Wesley (J.). Duty and Advantage of Early Rising. Ed. 2. 8º.

1786

Bible. 12⁰.
Common Prayer. 12⁰.
Isola (A.). Tasso, Gerusalemme Liberata. 8⁰.
Ogden (S.). Sermons. 2 vols. Ed. 3. 8⁰.
Ormerod (R.). Remarks on Priestley's Disquisitions. 8⁰.
Pickering (D.). Statutes. Vol. 35. 8⁰.
Purkis (W.). University Sermon. 4⁰.
Relhan (R.). Flora, Supplement 1. 8⁰.
Watson (R.). Chemical Essays. Vol. IV. 8⁰.

1787

Common Prayer. 12⁰.
Cooke (W.). Praelectio. 4⁰.
Graduati Cantabrigienses, 1659–1787. 4⁰.
Ludlam (W.). Mathematical Essays. Ed. 2. 8⁰.
    „   Rudiments of Mathematics. Ed. 2. 8⁰.
Morgan (C.). A Demonstration. 8⁰.
Nasmith (J.). Tanner's Notitia Monastica. F⁰.
Pickering (D.). Statutes. Vol. 36. 8⁰.
Relhan (R.). Heads of Lectures on Botany. 8⁰.
Watson (R.). Address to Young Persons. 8⁰.

1788

Act for paving...Cambridge. 8⁰.
Beausobre (I. de.) New version of St Matthew. 8⁰.
Beverley (J.). Ceremonies of the University. 8⁰.
Bible. 8⁰ and 12⁰.
Common Prayer. 4⁰.
Lettice (J.). Two Sermons. 4⁰.
Milner (I.). Plan of Chemical Lectures. 8⁰.
Parkinson (T.). Addenbrooke's Sermon. 4⁰.
[Peckard (P.).] Am I not a man and a brother? 8⁰.
Peckard (P.). University Sermon. 8⁰.
Relhan (R.). Flora, Supplement II.
Robinson (R.). Sermon on Slavery. 8⁰.
[Symonds (J.).] Reasons for revising the Bible. 8⁰.
Wakefield (G.). Virgil's Georgics. 8⁰.
Watson (R.). Address to Young Persons. 8⁰.
    „   Charge to the Clergy (Ely). 8⁰.
    „   Charge to the Clergy (Llandaff). 8⁰.
    „   Sermons and Tracts. 8⁰.

1789

Bible. F⁰ and 4⁰.
C., J. The Coin Act. 8⁰.
Common Prayer. 8⁰ and 12⁰.
Description of the Town and University. 12⁰.
Disney (W.). University Sermon. 4⁰.
Isola (A.). Ariosto, Orlando Furioso. 4 vols. 8⁰.
Mainwaring (J.). Sermon. 4⁰.

Morgan (C.). Sermon at Ely. 8⁰.
Parkinson (T.). Mechanics and Hydrostatics. 4⁰.
A Questionist. Address on W[illiam] F[rend's] Sermon. 8⁰.
Roberts (J.). The Deluge. 4⁰.
Seale (J. B.). Analysis of Greek Metres. Ed. 2. 8⁰.
Select Psalms. 8⁰.
Symonds (J.). Observations on revising the Gospels. 4⁰.
Wakefield (G.). Silva critica. Pt. I. 8⁰.

1790

Address to the National Assembly of France. 8⁰.
Beausobre (I. de). New Version of St Matthew. 8⁰.
Berkenhout (J.). Letters to his son. 8⁰.
Beverley (J.). Poll. 8⁰.
Bible. 12⁰.
Description of the Town and University. 12⁰.
Dickens (T.). Posthumous Poem. Ed. C. Dickens. 4⁰.
Edwards (T.). University Sermon. 4⁰.
Hey (J.). Sermon. 8⁰.
Labutte (R.). French Grammar. Ed. 2. 8⁰.
[Masters (R.).] Catalogue of Pictures in the University. 8⁰.
Peckard (P.). Memoirs of Nicholas Ferrar. 8⁰.
       ,,   University Sermon. 8⁰.
Philpot (C.). Faith, a Vision. 4⁰.
Pickering (D.). Statutes. Vol. 37. 8⁰.
Psalms. F⁰.
Stevens (T.). University Sermon (July). 4⁰.
       ,,   University Sermon (December). 4⁰.
Vince (S.). Treatise on Practical Astronomy. 4⁰.
Wakefield (G.). Silva critica. Pt. II. 8⁰.

1791

Bible. 12⁰.
Cockshutt (T.). Addenbrooke's Sermon. 4⁰.
Edwards (J.). Plutarch. 8⁰.
Fawcet (J.). Norrisian Prize Essay. 4⁰.
Hayter (T.). University Sermon. 8⁰.
Philpot (C.). Humility. 4⁰.

1792

Bible. 12⁰.
Carlyle (J. D.). Annales Rerum Aegypticarum. 4⁰.
Common Prayer. F⁰.
Excerpta e Statutis. 8⁰.
Favell (C.). Sermon. 4⁰.
Hey (J.). Heads of Lectures in Divinity. Ed. 2. 8⁰.
Jones (T.). University Sermon. 4⁰.
Marsh (H.). Discourse on Books of Moses. 4⁰.
       ,,   Essay on Theological Learning. 4⁰.
Oldershaw (J.). Sermon at Lambeth. 4⁰.

Seale (J. B.). University Discourse. 4⁰.
Thorp (R.). University Sermon. 4⁰.
Wakefield (G.). Silva critica. Pt. III. 8⁰.
Waring (E.). Algebraic Quantities. 8⁰.

1793

Atkins (J.). Treatise on the horizontal Sun. 8⁰.
[Bryant (J.).] Authenticity of the Scriptures. Ed. 2. 8⁰.
Falconer (W.). Tracts...relating to Natural History. 4⁰.
Fawcett (J.). Sermon. 4⁰.
Hey (J.). Heads of Lectures in Divinity. Ed. 2. 8⁰.
Kipling (T.). Codex Theodori Bezae. 2 vols. F⁰.
Marsh (H.). Michaelis. Introduction to N.T. Vols. 1 and 2. 8⁰.
Pearson (E.). Sermon. 8⁰.
Relhan (R.). Flora, Supplement III. 8⁰.
Vince (S.). Plan of Lectures on Natural Philosophy. 8⁰.

1794

Common Prayer. 12⁰.
Fawcett (J.). University Sermons. 8⁰.
Hey (J.). Heads of Lectures in Divinity. Ed. 3. 8⁰.
Milner (J.) History of the Church of Christ. Vol. 1. 8⁰.
Newton (T.). Conic Sections. 8⁰.
Owen (J.). Assize Sermon (March). 8⁰.
    „   Assize Sermon (August). 8⁰.
Pearson (E.). University Sermon. 8⁰.
Pickering (D.). Statutes. Vol. 39. 8⁰.
Randall (J.). Psalm and Hymn Tunes. 12⁰.
Symonds (J.). Observations on revising the Epistles. 4⁰.
Waring (E.). Essay on Human Knowledge. 8⁰.
Wollaston (F. J. H.). Plan of Chemical Lectures. 8⁰.

1795

Bible. 8⁰ and 12⁰.
Hallifax (S.). Heads of Lectures on Roman Law. Ed. 4. 8⁰.
Lettice (J.). Trans. of Browne's Immortality of the Soul. 8⁰.
Mainwaring (J.). University Sermon. 4⁰.
Milner (J.). History of the Church of Christ. Vol. II. 8⁰.
Pearson (E.). University Sermon (June). 8⁰.
    „   University Sermon (October). 8⁰.
Pickering (D.). Statutes. Vol. 40. 8⁰.
Ramsden (R.). University Sermon. 8⁰.
Thomason (T.). Norrisian Prize Essay. 8⁰.
Trollope (A. W.). The Destruction of Babylon. 4⁰.
Vince (S.). Principles of Fluxions. 8⁰.
Wood (J.). Elements of Algebra. 8⁰.
Wrangham (F.). The Restoration of the Jews. 4⁰.

1796

Benjoin (G.). Trans. of Jonah. 4⁰.
Carlyle (J. D.). Specimens of Arabian Poetry. 4⁰.

Common Prayer. 4º and 12º.
Coulthurst (H. W.). University Sermon. 8º.
Description of the Town and University. 12º.
Donn (J.). Hortus cantabrigiensis. 8º.
Farish (W.). Plan of Lectures in Arts and Manufactures. 8º.
Harwood (B.). Comparative Anatomy and Physiology. Vol. I. 4º.
Hey (J.). Lectures in Divinity. Vol. I. 8º.
Jerram (C.). Norrisian Prize Essay. 8º.
Pearson (E.). Sermon. 8º.
Plumptre (J.). Observations on Hamlet. 8º.
    ,,   Pope's Ecloga Sacra and Gray's Elegy in Greek. Ed. 2. 4º.
Ramsden (R.). University Sermon. 8º.
Simeon (C.). University Sermon. Ed. 4. 8º.
Vince (S.). Principles of Hydrostatics. 8º.
Wood (J.). Principles of Mechanics. 8º.

1797

Bible. 8º.
Bolland (W.). Miracles. 4º.
Bryant (J.). Sentiments of Philo-Judaeus. 8º.
Butler (S.). M. Musuri carmen. 8º.
Common Prayer. Fº.
Hey (J.). Lectures in Divinity. Vols. II and III. 8º.
Isola (A.). Italian Poetry. New ed. 8º.
Milner (J.). History of Church of Christ. Vol. III. 8º.
Newton (C.). Poems. 8º.
Pearson (E.). Four University Sermons. (Title only.) 8º.
Pickering (D.). Statutes. Vol. 41. 8º.
Plumptre (J.). Appendix to Observations on Hamlet. 8º.
Seale (J. B.). Addenbrooke's Sermon. 4º.
Simeon (C.). Assize Sermon. 8º.
Vince (S.). Complete System of Astronomy. Vol. I. 4º.
    ,,   Heads of Lectures on Experimental Philosophy. 8º.
Wilson (W.). Method of explaining N.T. 8º.

1798

Bible. 8º and 12º.
Clark (W.). Sermon. 4º.
Craven (W.). Addenbrooke's Sermon. 8º.
    ,,   The Jewish Dispensations. 8º.
Frere (B.). Poemata. ' 8º.
Green (A.). Norrisian Prize Essay. 8º.
Hardy (R.). University Sermon. 4º.
Hey (J.). Lectures in Divinity. Vol. IV. 8º.
Mainwaring (J.). Remarks on the Pursuits of Literature. 8º.
New Testament. 4º.
Ode au Roi de la Grande Bretagne. 4º.
Pearson (E.). Discourses to Academic Youth. 8º.
Seale (J. B.). Analysis of Greek Metres. Ed. 3. 8º.
Simeon (C.). University Sermon. Ed. 6. 8º.
Vince (S.). Two University Discourses. 8º.

Wall (A.). Senate House Ceremonies. 8°.
Wood (J.). Elements of Algebra. Ed. 2. 8°.

1799

Bolland (W.). The Epiphany. 4°.
Common Prayer. 12°.
Collignon (Cath.). Ladvocat's Biographical Dictionary. Vol. I. 8°.
Ingram (R. A.). Syllabus of Political Philosophy. 8°.
Making of Deacons and Ordering of Priests. 8°.
[Pearson (E.).] Letter to Member of Senate. 8°.
Pickering (D.). Statutes. Vol. 42. 8°.
Reynolds (T.). Iter Britanniarum. 4°.
Taylor (T. G.). Norrisian Prize Essay. 8°.
Vince (S.). Complete System of Astronomy. Vol. II. 4°.
„   Principles of Astronomy. 8°.
Wood (J.). Elements of Optics. 8°.
„   Principles of Mechanics. Ed. 2. 8°.

1800

Bolland (W.). St Paul at Athens. 4°.
Cantabrigienses Graduati, 1659–1800. 4°.
Collignon (Cath.). Ladvocat's Biographical Dictionary. Vol. II. 8°.
Craven (W.). Continuation of a Discourse. 8°.
Donn (J.). Hortus cantabrigiensis. Ed. 2. 8°.
Harraden (R.). Views of Cambridge. Oblong F°.
„   Description of Cambridge. 8°.
Hoogeveen (H.). Dictionarium Analogicum. 4°.
Luke (R.). University Sermon. 4°.
Milner (I.). Animadversions on Dr Haweis. 8°.
Milner (J.). History of the Church. Vol. I. Ed. 2. 8°.
Ramsden (R.). Commemoration Sermon. 8°.
„   University Sermon (January). 8°.
„   University Sermon (March). 8°.
Roberts (P.). Harmony of the Epistles. 4°.
Thomason (T.). Norrisian Prize Essay. 8°.
Uvedale (R.). Sermon. 4°.
Vince (S.). Conic Sections. Ed. 2. 8°.
„   Plane and Spherical Trigonometry. 8°.
„   Principles of Fluxions. Ed. 2. 8°.
„   Principles of Hydrostatics. Ed. 2. 8°.
Waterland (D.). Doctrine of the Holy Trinity. Ed. 3. 8°.
Wrangham (F.). The Holy Land. 4°.